"Face to Face with Jesus is a story I _ the unique and inspiring journey of coming to know Christ. This book _ ... _..... your life. Get ready."

Bill Johnson, senior leader, Bethel Church, Redding, CA; author, *When Heaven Invades Earth*; co-author, *The Essential Guide to Healing* and *Healing Unplugged*

"This is one of the most powerful testimonies to the reality and faithfulness of Jesus that I have ever read. You cannot come away from reading this book without being awed. As persecution of Christians by radical Muslims sweeps across the earth, Samaa Habib's testimony is a story that must be heard."

Joel Richardson, *New York Times* bestselling author, teacher

"Hard-hitting reality and deep intimacy with Messiah—Samaa's amazing story takes you into the thick of Islam's heartland. Watch how a traditional Muslim girl encounters a Middle Eastern Jesus, lives boldly for Him, suffers martyrdom and resuscitation and shines the light of God on her beloved people. This is a modern book of Acts that will help you fall more deeply in love with Yeshua."

Avner Boskey, Final Frontier Ministries

"This riveting story is a must-read for anyone who wants insights into the complexities of the Muslim world. It is a story filled with faith, hope and the power of the supernatural intervention of God. This book is destined to be a classic."

Mark Anderson, president, call2all

"In the midst of great opposition and unending persecution, Samaa takes us on a journey of heart-lifting hope. The depth of her prayer life and her resolute commitment to depend on Jesus will awaken you to know and share His matchless love—even in the toughest of circumstances."

Paul Eshleman, vice president of coverage, Campus Crusade for Christ International

"You will thrill at this true story of suffering and redemption, and like me, you will be riveted by Samaa's journey from a Muslim upbringing to a bold stand for Christ. For Muslims and Christians everywhere, this book will ignite your heart and strengthen your faith."

Bob Sorge, author, speaker; www.bobsorge.com

"You need to read this book. In all my years of ministry and being around countless people impacted by God's encountering them, this one takes me closer to the incredible reality of the goodness of Jesus, every time."

Eric Johnson, senior pastor, Bethel Redding; author, *Momentum: What God Starts Never Ends*

"Having traveled extensively across the Middle East for years, I can boldly testify that Samaa's story is a divine illustration of the widespread revelation of Jesus striking those lands in this hour! Let her testimony of this unstoppable Gospel shred every fear, break down every wall and remove all doubt in your life!"

Sean Feucht, author, recording artist, international speaker; founder, Burn 24-7

"Samaa's story deeply impacted my heart and my life. Her testimony is so alive with the power of the Gospel, so interwoven with the revelation and love of Jesus—such a fragrant life. I've never read a book like this before. You must read it!"

David Brymer, worship director, Pasadena International House of Prayer

"Samaa's story draws you in to her dramatic yet touching journey, giving you new eyes to see a world we rarely see. Intimate and bold, *Face to Face with Jesus* unveils God's concern and faithfulness to all who love and trust Him."

Chris DuPré, president, Heart of David Publishing

"Samaa is intensely passionate about the One who snatched her from death and darkness. Her story will ignite wholehearted faith and inject hope and courage to many. As the days of fire increase, His resurrection power and authority will become more manifest. The Bride of Christ will be made ready for His soon return. Maranatha!"

David Demian, director, Watchmen for the Nations

"This book has the potential to change your life. I know the author, and this testimony—her life—is one of the most amazing things I have ever witnessed. It proves the fact of God's love and zeal to see millions of Muslims come to a saving knowledge of Jesus Christ. Samaa Habib is a picture of what I believe God is beginning to do and will only increase in the days ahead. Get ready, because your life is about to be rocked!"

> Corey Russell, director, Forerunner Program,
> International House of Prayer University

"Samaa's testimony and heavenly encounter have stirred in me a renewed passion for Jesus and a burning conviction to bodly share His Gospel and love to all men. So compelling and encouraging to read!"

> Laura Hackett, singer/songwriter;
> worship leader, International House of Prayer

"*Face to Face with Jesus* is a captivating story of faith, courage and love and is a great treasure to Muslims and Christians alike. Muslims will hear the story of the Savior's unfailing, tender love, and Christians will be provoked to join Him in His mission to make it known."

> Allen Hood, associate director, International House of
> Prayer; president, International House of Prayer University

"*Face to Face with Jesus* not only is a testimony of courage beyond imagination but gives us a picture of everyday realities for the persecuted church. Every believer needs to read it with eyes wide open to the suffering of those who live amidst warring factions. Samaa Habib and Bodie Thoene have done us a huge favor in writing this book."

> Cindy Jacobs, Generals International

"A faith-building page-turner, this extraordinary story continuously 'shouts' the power of God's furious love for His children. The author's story has proven that for believers who go through an intense furnace of trials, God's faithfulness allows them to emerge with no trace of the smell of smoke. This book is absolutely a must-read!"

> Dr. Terri L. Terry, academic dean, Forerunner Music
> Academy, International House of Prayer University

"This story is the equivalent of Acts 29—the explosive power of the Gospel breaking in in the midst of persecution, threats of death and great opposition. Read Samaa Habib's story and you will break forth with hope and joy because the testimony of Jesus is the spirit of prophecy. God is coming to the Muslim world."

Lou Engle, founder, TheCall

"Within the pages of *Face to Face with Jesus* is a revelation of a Father who is passionately in pursuit of people and is awakening hearts with His power and love. Samaa's story will ignite within you a passion to pray and a faith to believe that with God nothing is impossible."

Banning Liebscher, director, Jesus Culture

"In *Face to Face with Jesus*, I am amazed by a small, once fearful Muslim girl who encounters the living God and is transformed into a mighty force. Horrifically persecuted for years, yet never denying Jesus, Samaa shares her powerful message of Christ's love and forgiveness for her oppressors. Let her life be our example."

Heidi Baker, founding director, Iris Global

"When I met this author and heard her story, I wept with love for the One who pursued her and gave her strength to endure the things she has endured for His sake. This story will move your heart in a profound way and inspire you in courage as well as in intercession that there would be many more like Samaa who will come to know Him no matter the cost."

Misty Edwards, senior leader and worship leader,
International House of Prayer

"In Samaa's story Jesus transforms her hopelessness into hope, and her trials become stepping-stones rather than stumbling blocks. Jesus has hopeful, overcoming plans for all His people. We see this walked out beautifully here in the journey of Samaa's life."

Bob Hartley, CEO and founder, Deeper Waters, Inc.,
and Hartley Group

FACE *to* FACE *with* JESUS

FACE *to* FACE *with* JESUS

A FORMER MUSLIM'S EXTRAORDINARY JOURNEY *to* HEAVEN AND ENCOUNTER *with* THE GOD OF LOVE

SAMAA HABIB

and BODIE THOENE

Research by Jemimah Wright

Chosen

a division of Baker Publishing Group
Minneapolis, Minnesota

© 2014 by Samaa Habib and Bodie Thoene

Published by Chosen Books
11400 Hampshire Avenue South
Bloomington, Minnesota 55438
www.chosenbooks.com

Chosen Books is a division of
Baker Publishing Group, Grand Rapids, Michigan

Printed in the United States of America

Library of Congress Cataloging-in-Publication Data
Habib, Samaa.
    Face to face with Jesus : a former Muslim's extraordinary journey to heaven and encounter with the God of love / Samaa Habib and Bodie Thoene ; foreword by Mike Bickle ; research by Jemimah Wright.
        pages cm
    Summary: "The thrilling and heart-wrenching true story of a former Muslim woman's journey to heaven and back when she was victim of a terrorist bombing"— Provided by publisher.
    ISBN 978-0-8007-9579-5 (pbk. : alk. paper)
    1. Habib, Samaa. 2. Christian biography. 3. Christianity and other religions—Islam. 4. Islam—Relations—Christianity. 5. Christian converts from Islam—Biography. I. Thoene, Bodie, II. Title.
BR1725.H155A3 2014
275.6′083092—dc23   2013047096

The song "The Battle Hymn of the Republic" mentioned in chapter 1 by Julia Ward Howe, 1861.

The song "All Heaven Declares" mentioned in chapter 8 by Tricia and Noel Richards, copyright © 1987 Thankyou Music (PRS).

The song "Worthy Is the Lamb" mentioned in chapter 8 by Darlene Zschech, copyright © 2000 Darlene Zschech/Hillsong Publishing.

The song "God Will Make a Way" mentioned in chapter 25 by Don Moen, copyright © 1990 Integrity's Hosanna! Music.

Unless otherwise indicated, Scripture quotations are from the New American Standard Bible®, copyright © 1960, 1962, 1963, 1968, 1971, 1972, 1973, 1975, 1977, 1995 by The Lockman Foundation. Used by permission.

Scripture quotations identified ESV are from The Holy Bible, English Standard Version® (ESV®), copyright © 2001 by Crossway, a publishing ministry of Good News Publishers. Used by permission. All rights reserved. ESV Text Edition: 2007

Scripture quotations identified NIV are from the Holy Bible, New International Version®. NIV®. Copyright © 1973, 1978, 1984, 2011 by Biblica, Inc.™ Used by permission of Zondervan. All rights reserved worldwide. www.zondervan.com

Scripture quotations identified NKJV are from the New King James Version. Copyright © 1982 by Thomas Nelson, Inc. Used by permission. All rights reserved.

Scripture quotations identified KJV are from the King James Version of the Bible.

Cover design by Gearbox/Dan Pitts

15   16   17   18   19   20   8   7   6   5   4

To My Dearly Beloved Lord and Savior, Jesus Christ!
To My Precious Mom and Dad, Siblings and Relatives
To the Faithful Persecuted Church

CONTENTS

Foreword by Mike Bickle   13

Acknowledgments   15

1. Explosion   17
2. Miracle Child   31
3. Growing Up Muslim   37
4. Civil War   49
5. Famine   57
6. The Holy Book   72
7. Tremendous Revelations   78
8. Encounter with Love   85
9. Walking with Jesus   95
10. Supernatural Strength   102
11. The Cost of Following Jesus   114
12. Supernatural Bodyguard   121

Contents

13. The Seeds Grow   129

14. The Old Becomes New   145

15. A Bold Faith   158

16. Salvation of the Household   166

17. Heaven   174

18. Fighting for My Life   183

19. Healing Miracles   188

20. Deliverance   206

21. Miraculous Transformations   213

22. Provision by Heavenly Provider   219

23. Acts of Faith   224

24. Go to the End of the Earth   237

25. Going to America   240

Epilogue: Four Dreams   257

FOREWORD

"In this world you will have tribulation. But take heart! I have overcome the world."

John 16:33 NIV

Jesus declared that believers will have trouble in this world, but that if we are faithful, we will overcome. The Body of Christ throughout history has endured persecution and great troubles. For many believers, particularly in the West, persecution is a foreign concept and experience—limited to unpleasant exchanges in the office or over social media. However, for many other believers, from Indonesia to Africa, in North Korea and throughout the Middle East, persecution is common. They suffer in many different ways, from social and economic exclusion to torture, rape, imprisonment and martyrdom for their belief in Jesus.

I am honored to know Samaa and have been encouraged by her faith in the Lord. She is one who has gone through the fiery trials of persecution, even to the point of death, and emerged on the other side, loving Jesus with even greater zeal. Her story is one of great endurance and perseverance. She has endured many fiery trials so that she, along with others, may echo Paul's prayer:

> . . . that I may know Him and the power of His resurrection, and the fellowship of His sufferings, being conformed to His death, if, by any means, I may attain to the resurrection from the dead.
>
> Philippians 3:10–11 NKJV

Reading this story is like reading the book of Acts. I encourage you to read. I believe you will be inspired to go deeper in a life of prayer, not only to deepen your own spiritual history in the Lord but also to connect your life of prayer to the global persecuted church and really to "Remember the prisoners as if chained with them—those who are mistreated—since you yourselves are in the body also" (Hebrews 13:3 NKJV). As the Church draws closer to the return of the Lord, more and more believers will be persecuted and will need to understand what it is to be an overcoming and faithful church. Let Samaa's story inspire you to be faithful and help connect you with the heart of Jesus and the persecuted Church globally.

Mike Bickle,
director, International House of Prayer

ACKNOWLEDGMENTS

My deepest appreciation and sincere gratitude to my heavenly Father for His unfailing love, to our Lord Jesus for His amazing grace and to the Holy Spirit, whose fellowship and guidance is a tremendous help throughout life and during this project!

From the bottom of my heart I would like to thank Jemimah Wright, who inspired me to write this book and helped so much with the first manuscript. You are a "brilliant" servant of the Lord.

Bodie and Brock Thoene, very humble servants of the Lord, God brought us together. Your skillfulness and creativity is what has brought this project to its beautiful completion. Without you, it would not have happened. I am so grateful. You are such a wonderful blessing.

Ramona Tucker, your deft touch, sweetness and professionalism have added so much to the manuscript. Thank you.

Jane Campbell, a woman of virtue with the fear of the Lord; Carra Carr, who assisted in choosing the name of the book, the design and marketing, and all the amazing team at Chosen

Books: Thank you so much for believing in this project and encouraging my heart.

Jono Hall, you are a peacemaker and have wisdom beyond your years. Thank you.

Thank you to all the shepherds, missionaries and generals of faith who have guided me in the love of God throughout the years, including my original pastors from the Middle East, Paul Eshleman, Mike Bickle, Bill Johnson, Mark Anderson, John Dawson and everyone in the global Prayer and Missions movement. I am walking on your shoulders.

Thank you to all the beloved "darling" intercessor friends who have stood with me through the entire writing process and supported me.

Explosion

And they overcame him because of the blood of the Lamb and because of the word of their testimony, and they did not love their life even when faced with death.

Revelation 12:11

Death was not on my mind when I awakened that sunny fall morning in the capital city of my Middle Eastern homeland. Terrorists and bombs that would tear my world to pieces were as far from my thoughts as east is from west.

I was nineteen years old. Life and joy and the ordinary hopes of a young woman filled my heart.

Light streamed through the window of my bedroom and penetrated my eyelids. I opened my eyes and lay quietly listening to the stirring of life in my home. Birds sang outside my window. I was happy that it was Sunday, my favorite day of the week. From the kitchen I heard my father's hearty laughter.

My mother was visiting my grandmother for three days, so my sisters took over the tasks of preparing breakfast.

"Samaa," my sister called, "are you awake?"

"Almost." I sat up on the edge of my bed. "Good morning, Lord," I whispered. "Thank You for this beautiful autumn day. I give every moment to You."

As if to interrupt my sweet conversation with Jesus, the loudspeaker on the minaret of the local mosque broadcast the insistent call of the muezzin, summoning the faithful Muslims of our neighborhood to prayer.

My father was a lawyer, a respected Ph.D. professor of philosophy at the university and also a Mullah, a religious leader and teacher. That morning, as I dressed, I heard him go to his room and pray the ritual prayers to Allah. I knew he tried to ignore the disgrace he felt that some of his family had converted from Islam to follow Jesus Christ.

My father knew I would be going to church. Six of his ten children, as well as my mother, had accepted Christ. My mother was well educated, knew three different languages and had been a professor of language at the school before giving all that up to marry my father and become the honored mother of ten children. I was the youngest daughter.

Our conversion to Christ was deeply troubling to my father.

As Muslim prayers penetrated my door I quietly prayed for him, "Lord, I ask that You lift the veil of spiritual blindness for my dear father so that he, too, may truly know the joy of salvation through Your Son, Jesus. Reveal to him that Jesus is not only a Prophet but the Son of the Living God."

I decided to wear high heels and a new ankle-length green and gray dress that had been a present from a friend. I brushed my long brown hair, making sure I looked my best for the Lord. I didn't want to be late.

I hugged my brothers and sisters good morning and kissed them. "I have to be at church early."

"You need to eat breakfast," my sister said firmly, offering me a cup of tea.

I drank it quickly before grabbing a pomegranate from a bowl. "No time for more. I'm singing in the choir and want to visit with Adila before practice."

Father entered the kitchen. "Give your sister Adila my love. Bring her home. Why should she stay at the church when she has a home and a mother and father?"

"I will tell her, Papa. But you know it's part of her schooling."

Adila was only a year older than me. Tall and beautiful, she had returned from Bible school in Europe and was living at our church while receiving practical training.

> **Those good shepherds who had founded our church courageously chose to stay with their flock.**

"Tell her I love her. And I love you, too, my darling daughter," Papa said.

I blew him a kiss as I ran out the door.

"Be safe, my precious girl," he shouted after me. At that moment, did my father somehow sense the ordeal that lay ahead? Only two days earlier, the U.S. Embassy had evacuated its personnel in response to "a confirmed terrorist threat against foreigners." Some resident foreigners had been informed of the threat by Islamic extremists, but those good shepherds who had founded our church courageously chose to stay with their flock.

I did not personally feel a threat from terrorists. Instead, my church had been the target of harassment by government officials. The Committee for Religious Affairs threatened to revoke the church's registration because we held evangelistic outreaches in the capital. Three times in the previous year police had raided worship meetings and arrested people during services, confiscating our literature and handing down punishments for "illegal missionary propaganda."

Yet we were all unafraid. The joy and peace of Jesus, which passes all understanding, filled our hearts and minds. We were convinced of the Lord's promise to never leave us or forsake us. Though my mother and father might have been afraid for us, their children, I felt no fear. If God was for us, who could be against us?

I hurried out the door of our apartment and raised my face to the sunlight. "Lord, show my dear father how much You love him and how much You love us, Your children. Let Papa experience the joy of salvation we do."

As I walked, heels clicking on the pavement, I felt that Jesus walked beside me. The air was scented with the aroma of cooking breakfast and the muskiness of autumn leaves.

My Island of Hope

After several long blocks I spotted the three-story complex of dormitories and offices housing our rented building. This was my spiritual home, an island of hope in the midst of a sea of spiritual darkness.

My nation was 98 percent Muslim, and though we were a land that aspired to democracy, freedom of religion was an idea, not the reality of our lives. We had only recently survived a brutal civil war, which ended up as a religious war between the two main denominations of Islam—Sunni Muslims and Shia Muslims—who had divided after the death of the Prophet Muhammad over issues of who should be the next leader. The word *Sunni* in Arabic comes from a word meaning "one who follows the traditions of the Prophet." The Sunni believed their leader should be elected from among those capable of the job and thus the Prophet Muhammad's advisor, Abu Bakr, became the first caliph of the Islamic nation. The word *Shia* in Arabic means "a group or supportive party of people." The Shia believed leadership should have passed directly to his cousin and son-in-law, Ali (in other words, people in Muhammad's household). As a result, the two groups had slaughtered one another for years, leaving over 100,000 dead and many more crippled for life. The civil war was supposed to be a war for freedom, but only one thing united the Sunni and Shia Muslims: hatred of Christians and Jews. One could be "born" a Christian and that was tolerated, but those Muslims who converted to Christ and turned from the Qur'an to the Bible were considered by radical Muslims to be traitors, worthy of a horrible death.

As I stepped onto the holy ground I smiled and breathed a sigh of relief. I always felt safe there because of the presence of the Lord.

As I stepped onto the holy ground I smiled and breathed a sigh of relief. I always felt safe there because of the presence of the Lord.

Hurrying to my sister's dorm room in the complex I was surprised to find her still in bed. Her dark eyes were cloudy with fever.

"Adila? Are you sick?" I sank beside her and put my hand on her forehead. She was burning up.

She blinked at me and replied weakly, "I've had a terrible night."

"What's wrong?" The color had drained from her beautiful olive skin. I laid my hands on her head and prayed for her healing. Then I gave her the pomegranate I brought from home.

She whispered, "Don't tell Mother or Father I'm ill. They'll worry."

"All right, darling. I'm so sorry. Just try to sleep awhile. I've got to go to choir practice. After the service I'll come back, bring you tea and pray without ceasing for you. I'll ask the choir to pray for you, too."

My sister nodded and lay back on the pillow, closing her eyes. "Thank you. Yes. Keep praying, please."

Hurrying across the courtyard to the adjoining building, I outran the fallen leaves swirling on the breeze. Dashing into the basement practice room, I grabbed my choir robe from the rack and pulled it on.

"Samaa! You're on time!" called my friend Wafa, meaning "Faithful,"* a cheerful boy about my age. He had been to Bible school with my sister Adila and was a good friend. Because he was an only child and did not have sisters, he was like a little brother to us.

Embraced by my friends, I was laughing as I straightened the purple cross embroidered on the front of the white gown. I laughed again as the futility of my actions became clear. Greeting friends and family on the cheek with the traditional three kisses, as well as hugging them, rearranged every pleat and fold.

Arriving even later than me, my sister Iman joined me in the middle of our section. She came in time to begin our warm-up exercises. I also asked the choir to pray together for Adila's recovery. As two or three gather in the name of the Lord, He is in the midst of us and will grant us what we ask in agreement.

We left the basement and climbed the narrow stairs to the third-floor sanctuary. The choir seats were at the front, beneath a large wooden cross mounted on the wall, and ahead of wooden benches occupied by nearly five hundred people.

A Riveting Message

Our pastor was away, so an assistant pastor would be preaching while my good friend Missionary Johnny, meaning "God Is Gracious," would lead the worship.

*In my culture, as well as in Bible times, the meanings of names are important. That is why I will be mentioning these throughout this book.

We sang "Hallelujah," "God Is So Good" and "Praise the Lord!" We sang about His love and His glory and His majesty. My spirit soared with joy and shivered with the intensity of it. There was delight on the faces of those gathered together. "The joy of the Lord is my strength, and my light and my salvation," we sang, and I knew it was true.

In between songs Missionary Johnny told inspiring stories of God's faithfulness and blessings poured out on believers around the world. But when a shadow crossed his face, I knew something was troubling him.

When he spoke again, he related a story about a missionary in China. The man had been persecuted for his faith and then physically attacked. When he finally escaped to go home, it was in a wheelchair. The man's nose had also been cut off.

My sister Iman, next to me, gasped in horror.

Missionary Johnny went on: "It's not a happy message, but the Lord has told me that persecution is going to come. We need to be ready for it. Jesus was persecuted in His life. He suffered, and so will we. Are you ready to be persecuted for Him? Are you ready to die for Him?"

There was such urgency and anguish in his voice that I wondered if he had been tormented by a dream or vision, pressuring him to deliver this question with fervor. He certainly held the attention of everyone in the room. It was so quiet I could hear birds singing through the glass of the windows lining both sides of the packed sanctuary.

When Missionary Johnny sat down, the assistant pastor approached the lectern. He began his message with a Scripture reading.

"When Jesus came into the district of Caesarea Philippi," he quoted from Matthew 16, "He was asking His disciples, 'Who do people say that the Son of Man is?'

"And they said, 'Some say John the Baptist; and others, Elijah; but still others, Jeremiah or one of the prophets.'

"He said to them, 'But who do you say that I am?'

"Simon Peter answered, 'You are the Christ, the Son of the living God.'

"And Jesus said to him, 'Blessed are you, Simon Barjona, because flesh and blood did not reveal this to you, but My Father who is in heaven. I also say to you that you are Peter (which means 'rock'), and upon this rock I will build My church; and the gates of Hades will not overpower it. I will give you the keys of the Kingdom of heaven; and whatever you bind on earth shall have been bound in heaven, and whatever you loose on earth shall have been loosed in heaven' (verses 13–19)."

> **"Will you be brave enough, even if you think you might be persecuted, to say . . . 'He is the Christ, the Son of the living God'?"**

The preacher paused before he asked, "When someone says to you, 'Who is this Jesus you speak of? Who is He?' will you be brave enough, even if you think you might be persecuted, to say, like Peter did: 'He is the Christ, the Son of the living God'?"

Setting the idea of persecution against the promises we had heard, I pondered the notion that hell cannot triumph over us and cherished again the remembrance of Christ's victory over death. I felt a return of the joy and contentment with which the morning had begun.

After the sermon, we took an offering. I happened to glance at the wall clock at the back. It was a few minutes before midday. Iman left the front of the room to get the flowers we always give to welcome newcomers.

At the director's signal, the choir stood for the next hymn and began to sing "The Battle Hymn of the Republic." The words

"Glory, glory, hallelujah" rang in the chamber as we lifted our voices in my favorite hymn. I found such power and confidence in the marching beat, the stirring chords and the praise-filled words.

My soul was once more back in the grip of the joy of worshiping my Jesus when suddenly there was a flash of light and a deafening roar!

The whole building shook, as if there had been an earthquake, and I grasped the back of my chair to keep from falling. I was deafened by the noise, like a thousand trumpets blasting together. . . .

Pandemonium

The entire auditorium was suddenly cloaked with dense black smoke. There was a commotion in the middle of the room, but I couldn't make out the cause or the result. It felt as though I was under water or my ears were stuffed with cotton. The stench of the fumes made me cough and caused my eyes to burn.

All around voices babbled, "What happened? Is anyone hurt? What do we do?"

Trying to peer through the cloud of debris and fumes, I shouted for Iman: "Are you all right?" Then I remembered she was no longer nearby. Like many others, I kept asking, "What was that?"

"I don't know," each person replied.

I thought, *Maybe this is the Second Coming of Jesus?* Could it be? Could this clamor be the Lord's return? As I peered into the unnatural gloom and strained my ringing ears, the words of Revelation came to my lips as a prayer: "The Spirit and the bride say, 'Come'" (22:17). Then, without thinking about it, I started singing the hymn. When I looked around, many in the choir were raising their hands and singing with me, too. They joined me in saying, "Amen! Come, Lord Jesus, come!"

Was it possible? Was Jesus calling us home right now?

I felt no fear and had no sense of danger, only confusion. If there was no spiritual explanation, then perhaps it had been an accident.

Maybe this was the Second Coming of Jesus?

The air began to clear a little, and I noticed windows had been shattered. I heard shouting but could not comprehend the words.

Ever since the civil war my country had experienced many electrical and mechanical equipment problems. Maybe what had happened was merely caused by an electrical fault.

That notion was dispelled when a member of the congregation, who was in our country's military, ran toward the front, waving his arms and shouting, "Get out. Get out, now! It was a bomb! There may be more. Hurry!"

Pandemonium struck. People screamed in fear. The only exit, at the back of the room, was jammed with church members trying to fight their way out. Five hundred bodies tried to exit through a doorway barely big enough for two at a time.

Caught in the surge, I felt myself carried toward the rear of the chamber. Even if I had wanted to turn, I couldn't have done so. My other siblings were not present, and Adila was sick in her room, but where was Iman? She had gone to get the flowers, but now I couldn't see her anywhere!

When I got to the middle of the auditorium, I gasped. There was a hole in the floor over three feet wide! Benches and chairs were splintered from the blast, and bodies lay atop the sticks. Everything near the explosion had been completely destroyed. There was a hole in the roof.

When the fumes cleared still more, I witnessed other people

lying wounded and bleeding amid the wreckage. Groans and cries for help mingled with the noises of panicked worshipers trying to escape. Others began the grim task of aiding the injured.

Aishah, a dear friend who danced with me on the worship dance team, clasped her hands to her stomach. She was trying to walk, but blood seeped out between her clenched fingers. She did not speak, but her eyes flashed me a terrified appeal.

Grabbing her around her shoulders, I helped her toward the stairs, but it was like dragging a weighted sack. She could not make her feet move, and she swayed as if she would collapse any second.

It looked as though my friends were dying all around me, and there was nothing I could do!

I stumbled toward a wooden bench, now broken in two and propped up at a crazy angle. Blood

"God help us," I whispered. I sensed an answering breath of supernatural peace.

was spattered everywhere like scarlet paint. I had to get my friend out, had to get her help, but the exit seemed no nearer than before. Were we moving at all? I began to think I was never going to be able to leave the building.

"God help us," I whispered. I sensed an answering breath of supernatural peace, but my body still shook from the shock of the horrifying sights and sounds.

Oily black dust settled on shattered furniture and shards of window glass. I choked and coughed, trying to cover my mouth with one hand and support my friend with the other. Nightmarish images of death, blood and horrible wounds crowded in, and I could not shut them out.

I needed air. Easing my friend onto what remained of the bench, I moved toward the fragmented remains of a windowsill.

A voice in my ear urged me to lean over and look at the sidewalk below.

"Jump," the voice whispered. "It's best. If you stay here, you'll choke to death . . . or burn to death . . . or be trampled. Jump!"

I knew it was the devil, tempting me to commit suicide. The building was so high that a fall of three stories would kill me instantly. But since God had given me life, I knew only He had the right to take it from me. I took authority over the spirit of suicide. *Satan, I rebuke you. Be gone in the name of Jesus!*

At that moment I spotted Missionary Johnny's wife trying to climb out an adjacent window. Her face was streaked with soot and blood, and she looked terrified. She wavered on the brink, with one foot already on the window ledge.

I caught her just in time. "Don't!" I said gently. "We'll be okay. We can get down the stairs now."

Falling into my arms, she cried and nodded. Already two others were helping my friend Aishah with the stomach wound, so I continued to assist Johnny's wife. We made it to the exit, stumbling over lost shoes, discarded purses and backpacks as we descended to the second floor.

Nodding her thanks, Johnny's wife, now calm, turned to help someone else.

On the landing to the second floor someone called my name. "Samaa! Help us!" An arm waved at me through a partly open door that led to the dark corridor. "There are lots of us in here. Our clothes were burned off by the blast."

In my culture it is shameful to be seen unclothed. The women would not allow themselves to be seen in that condition, even if it cost them their lives.

"Samaa, please save us! Get us something to cover our bodies," one woman pleaded on all of their behalf.

Stripping my choir robe off, I thrust it into the closet. "This will do for one," I instructed. "I'll get more and be right back."

I thought of Adila's room in the adjacent building. There I could borrow more clothing and check on her at the same time.

Once outside I spotted Adila running toward me. "Thank God, you're all right!" she cried, hugging me fiercely.

"I'm fine," I replied, "but I can't stop. There's no time." Briefly I explained, and together we ran back to her room to swoop up an armload of clothing. Kicking off my high heels, I tied my hair back and slipped on flat shoes so I could run faster. "There are lots more in need," I said.

"Next door," Adila urged. "Blankets and sheets and towels."

Toting large bundles, we sprinted back toward the bombed building. Wounded, bleeding and broken bodies were being carried outside the wreckage and laid in rows alongside the walls. Then I saw Iman! She was fine. She was helping. There was only time enough for a quick hug.

"I will stay and help the injured," Adila said.

"I'll take the clothes and come back," I told her.

✳

When Iman saw me go back into the building, she wanted to go, too, but felt the Holy Spirit tell her not to go. At first she ignored the prompting, but then felt Him caution her one more time. This time she obeyed and stayed outside, helping Adila with the wounded.

✳

Now I felt I was fighting my way upstream. So was my friend Wafa, who was helping to evacuate the wounded. So many panicked people were still struggling to escape from the building that it was impossible for us to get back up to the second floor. We got stuck in the stairwell between floors, waiting for the downward crush to subside.

The bundle of blankets, sheets and towels was so heavy that I leaned against a wall box containing a fire extinguisher. Catching my breath, I glanced at my watch. It had been thirty minutes since the detonation. Sabir, another friend, stepped toward me. He had been helping carry the wounded outside, and his shirt was covered with blood.

"Are you okay?" I asked and reached to touch his shoulder in comfort.

At that instant another bomb, hidden inside the fire extinguisher cabinet, exploded.

I was thrown ten feet into the air and smashed against the opposite wall. All the air was knocked out of me. I was deafened and blinded, yet at the same moment my entire body felt like it was on fire—like I had an electric shock coursing over me and through me.

The pain was excruciating. It felt like the angel of death was choking me. I was fighting for my breath.

The Bible says in Romans 10:13 that everyone who calls on the name of the Lord will be saved. I could not speak, but my heart cried out, *Jesus! Jesus, help me! Jesus, save me!* I gasped, and then I breathed my last.

Then all went black as my spirit left my body.

2

MIRACLE CHILD

In the 1980s, when I was born, my country was still under the control of the Communists.

Although Mama and Papa grew up in a Communist country, they followed the Muslim culture. A large family was a sign of great blessing from Allah. Before they married, their families had been friends. They had known one another as they were growing up.

My mother's sister had married my father's uncle, and they suggested that Ibraheem and Sarah, whose name meant "Princess," might be a perfect match. My grandparents agreed. After all, my father was an intelligent man and was studying for his Ph.D. in philosophy. As their daughter was clever, too, they wisely wanted an equal partner for her.

Even so, it was a love match. Mama was twenty and Papa thirty when they married in the 1960s. Papa felt he had found a treasure since my mother was acclaimed for her beauty and intelligence. Mama taught English at the school but gave it up when she married my father. She dedicated her life to him in the hopes of bearing Ibraheem many children—just as his name, which meant "father of multitudes," declared.

Both of my parents considered children a blessing from Allah and therefore wanted as many as possible. They tried to have children for three years, but there were no offspring. People began to whisper that they were cursed. After all, it's a curse in the Muslim culture to be barren.

After three years, my mother gave birth to a boy, and there was a huge celebration. My father named the boy *Daniyal*, which means "God is my judge." But the joy of his arrival soon came to a tragic end. Daniyal was not well. He died at the age of three months after an operation on his stomach. This was devastating for my mother and father. The gossip declared that they were indeed cursed. Mama lost all hope, heartbroken at the loss of her baby.

But the next year the heartache came to an end with the birth of my brother Suleyman, meaning "Peace." This was quickly followed by the arrival of eight more children: my brother Musa ("Drawn out of the water, Deliver"), sister Mubarak ("Blessed One"), brother Dawud ("Beloved"), sisters Muqaddas ("Holy, sacred"), Iman ("Faith"), Malika ("Queen"), Adila ("Righteous, just") and me.

From the time I was in the womb there had been a battle to end my life. Adila had been born only a year before me. My mother carried her and delivered her with ease.

I was a different story.

Mama's Battle

Mama's petite body was in pain almost constantly, she told me later, as I grew within her. Her arms and legs swelled terribly.

The government hospital of our city was staffed by trained

doctors and medical personnel, but no ultrasound was available. My parents had no idea if I was a girl or a boy, but from the way my mother carried me, friends guessed I was a girl. Being Muslim, my father hoped I would be a boy. He was already the father of five girls and only had three surviving boys. In the religion of Islam, daughters were not valued as highly as sons.

In spite of her discomfort, my mother carried me to full term. Early one Sunday morning the contractions began and rapidly increased in intensity. My father fed broth to one-year-old Adila, promising her, "We will return with a brand-new baby brother or sister for you. Whatever Allah wills."

She was too young to understand the words, but my siblings knew and all hoped for another baby boy.

My thirteen-year-old brother, Suleyman, remarked, "Mama, please bring home a baby brother. We boys are outnumbered."

"I'll do my best." Mama laughed.

After my parents hugged them good-bye, Suleyman was left in charge. Papa helped my mother down the stairs from their second-story apartment into the bustling streets. They traveled by taxi to the hospital as the pain of her contractions increased.

My father was smiling when they arrived at the hospital. The curse of barrenness had certainly come to an end!

Mama was examined immediately when they arrived at the maternity ward and quickly taken to the delivery room. My father was not permitted to go with her, because men were not allowed to be present at a child's birth, so he waited patiently outside the building. The weather was warm and pleasant. After experiencing the routine nine times before, Papa believed the delivery would happen quickly. He kept his attention fixed on the window, waiting for a nurse to appear and present his new-born child to him.

In the delivery room, the Communist midwife examined my mother and tried to feel the head of the baby. She seemed concerned. Speaking in the official language of the country instead of our native tongue to the other nurse, she said, "We should get rid of it. A tumor, I think. Not a baby."

She did not realize my mother was fluent in three languages and understood every terrifying word. Mama raised her head and commanded in the same language, "Don't you touch my baby!"

Though the midwife was shocked at Mama's response, she instructed, "Madam, it will be better if we abort whatever is inside you."

My mother was not convinced. Since she had already given birth nine times, she knew without a shadow of a doubt that she had a healthy baby inside her. So she argued with the midwife. "There's nothing wrong with my baby. I will not permit you to abort my child!"

"Don't you touch my baby!"

"Madam, I deliver babies every day, and I tell you this is not a baby, but a growth of some sort."

Beads of sweat trickled down Mama's face. The pain of the contractions was almost unbearable, but she would not give up or give in to the midwife. She had almost no strength, and my father was not permitted to be with her. This was a battle Mama had to fight on her own.

"If it is a baby, it is most certainly turned wrong," the midwife said. "Upside down in the womb. It will not survive, and if we do not act soon, you will die."

"Get someone else." Mama panted. "Another doctor. You will not kill my baby!"

The two women exchanged exasperated looks and left to call a Jewish midwife who was renowned in our country for her skill. They were concerned that they not be blamed if my mother died. My father was, after all, a lawyer and a man of influence in the city.

Within moments of the Jewish doctor's arrival in the room and a quick examination, the problem was discovered. I was face up in the birth canal, instead of the proper position of face down. Worse, I was stuck high in the canal, unable to drop. It was not surprising that Mama's labor was the worst she had ever experienced.

The Jewish doctor grasped the danger immediately. "If we are going to save the baby and the mother, we must perform a C-section."

Mama protested, still certain the staff intended to kill me. She was placed under general anesthetic and, within minutes, I was plucked from her womb at 3:00 p.m. that Sunday afternoon.

I immediately began to wail. I was definitely human, and it was too late for anyone to take my life. I believe I was saved by God for a purpose. My survival was due to the skill of a Jewish doctor in a Communist hospital staffed by Muslims.

My father was summoned as Mama recovered from the surgery and anesthetic. He was the first to hold me in his arms as Mama recovered.

> **My survival was due to the skill of a Jewish doctor in a Communist hospital staffed by Muslims.**

When Mama awakened, her first words were, "Ibraheem! How is my baby? Where is my baby?"

I was laid in her arms. She wept when she saw that I was alive. "My miracle child," she murmured.

In my culture, when a son is born, there is much celebrating in the hospital. Doctors and nurses come to congratulate the mother; relatives bring gifts of money and food. That was not the case for me. Only my mother and father rejoiced. They were to be pitied. After all, they had too many girls. Yet in spite of the fact that I was a female, my mother and father looked down at me with a tender love. Mama told me later that her eyes misted with tears as she studied my face and realized how very close they had come to losing me.

Mama was 37 years old when I was born. Her recuperation from the traumatic birth meant an eight-day stay in the hospital. My sisters rejoiced when, at last, word arrived that their baby sister was coming home with Mama.

My eldest sister, Mubarak, was nine years old. She was so excited about my arrival that she ran to all the neighbors, dancing and exclaiming, "Mama has a beautiful baby girl! They are coming home today!"

When she found my brothers Suleyman and Musa, they were outside playing soccer. They pretended they did not care. "Just another girl," they muttered.

My brothers and sisters soon fell in love with me, however. I was like a little doll to them and to their friends. With such a difficult beginning, perhaps I was treasured all the more. Here is the proof that I was loved: Of all the children in my family, my father only insisted on naming two of us—their first, son Daniyal, and me, the last daughter.

He called me Mariam, which means "Love."

To my mother, I was always her "miracle child."

3

GROWING UP MUSLIM

I was brought up in a blend of two cultures: Middle Eastern and Western. My homeland was westernized because of the influence of modern industrial cultures. Orthodox Christians and Jews lived in our neighborhood, but the vast majority of our people were born Muslim, which meant they were expected to remain faithful to the Islamic beliefs and the Qur'an for their lifetimes. It is written in the Qur'an that if a Muslim leaves Islam and converts to any other religion, the penalty is death. I understood from an early age that, because I was born a Muslim, I would die a Muslim.

Both Sunni and Shia women wore veils but were not required to cover their faces. Many women in rural areas wore the traditional blue, black or white veils. In the towns and cities it was more common for women to wear the colorfully embroidered traditional dresses that reached to ankles and wrists.

The Middle-Eastern influence was predominant in my family. During meals we sat on long cushions on the floor and ate with our right hand—the same hand we used to greet people. We never used our left for eating or greeting, since the left hand is used to clean the body and is therefore unclean. There was always an abundance of food—heaping platters of lamb kebabs, pita bread, grilled vegetables, tabouleh; soups; baklava for dessert with tea and fresh and dry fruits. We were very family oriented and ate all our meals together in conversation, joy and laughter. Our discussions lasted for hours and ranged from politics to school and sports.

I was the baby of my family, spoiled and lavished with love. I was treated as a treasure by my brothers and sisters.

During those early years, I knew only peace and security. I missed my five older sisters when they left for school each day, but played with girls my age from our apartment building. Orthodox Christians, Jewish and Muslim—we kids got along. I did not understand the divisions of religion and politics that separated the adults from one another.

My best friend was my sister Adila. When she was at school, my favorite playmate was a curly-haired girl named Gamila, meaning "Beautiful," who lived in the apartment close to us with her Sunni Muslim family. During long, cold winter months, when the wind howled down from the mountains, we frolicked in the snow or passed our hours playing in her apartment or mine. Our doors were not locked in the daylight hours, and we often ran between our two homes, giggling and chattering.

Gamila's mother was Mama's friend. She was a plump, sweet woman who loved to cook as the radio blared the traditional music of our country. She let Gamila and me help make huge meals for her family, so at a young age I learned to make bread and all my favorite meals.

My mother taught us our alphabet, how to read stories and the basics of the English language.

School Days

I was excited when I was old enough to start kindergarten. I tried on the European-style black-and-white school uniform my sisters had all worn in their early school years. Mama looked me over and said, "You are the last girl, and I think you've worn enough hand-me-downs from your sisters. Come along, Mariam, let's go shopping."

That day Mama took me shopping for my own brand-new school uniform. We boarded the bus together and she let me sit by the window, but instead of gazing at the passing sights, I turned and looked up at Mama. She was so pretty. Her thick dark hair was covered and a brightly embroidered scarf framed her oval face. Joy radiated in her eyes as she held my hand.

On this day, all was well as the crowded bus rumbled through the peaceful streets. I felt like my mother's only child. We stepped off the bus onto the sidewalk, and Mama smiled down at me. "What a big girl you are! Your first school uniform. What do you think, Mariam? What would you like to be when you grow up?"

I squeezed her hand. "I want to be just like you, Mama. I want to learn everything and speak English and teach like you."

She laughed and addressed me in English. "Thank you."

"You are welcome," I replied.

She laughed again, and I knew I had pleased her. That was my goal in life: to please my mother, father and grandma in all I did.

My mom wanted to travel to English-speaking nations like England and America. I'd tell her, "Great, Mama! Take me with you, and we can practice our English there." I would tell my father I wanted to be a lawyer—like him. My grandma wanted me to be a doctor. Many of my relatives were doctors or lawyers, too, or on their way to becoming such. I knew from my parents that the way to my dreams was through education.

On the first day of school, Mama brushed and braided my hair. My oldest sister, Mubarak, helped her. I stood in a stair-step line with my five sisters for examination.

"Beautiful!" Mama shook her head in wonder.

Papa crossed his arms. "Six girls. A good start on my own all-female soccer team." He placed his big hands on our heads in blessing. "Mariam, you are going to be the striker. Do you understand what I mean?"

"I think so. Always run fast?"

I was full of energy. I loved to run. Everywhere I went, I ran. In the morning, after our family breakfast, I'd run out of the house with the backdrop of my mother calling, "Don't run, Mariam, don't run!" ringing in my ears.

> "Everything you do should be done to play the game fairly and win the prize. Make the goal for the honor of all the team."

He laughed big. "Something like that. Adila," he addressed my sister, "can you explain?"

Though she was only a year older than me, Adila liked to be considered much wiser. "The striker makes the goal. Papa means that everything you do should be done to play the game fairly and win the prize. Make the goal for the honor of all the team."

"That is correct." Papa lowered his chin. "Try your hardest."

"I will, Papa," I answered. "I will try."

My father always called me a princess, believing in me and encouraging and inspiring me. He and my mom taught me that whatever I dreamed to be, I would accomplish it.

After hugs and kisses all around, we were off like a flock of geese to school, which was only a few minutes' walk from our apartment. My friends Gamila and Munira, meaning "Bright and Shining," joined us, and we felt very grown-up and confident with our new classmates.

From that first day, I caught the meaning of Papa's admonition to always stay out in front. Honoring and pleasing my parents was my motivation for everything. I loved school, enjoyed academics and was continually at the top of my class, which consisted of both boys and girls. Only in Islamic religious instruction were boys and girls in different classes.

I also excelled in sports and became the captain of the sports teams. I especially loved basketball, volleyball and gymnastics. I learned traditional dances as well as ballet. I was so physically active that I ran almost everywhere. More than once I tumbled and needed stitches, but I never broke a bone. I became a natural leader and easily invited friends to join me in whatever sport or game I was playing.

Even though I was doing well in school and continued to be popular with my peers, deep in my heart I had a desire for something more in my life. I not only wanted to please my parents, I wanted to know and please God. I was desperate to hear Allah's voice, but he never spoke to me.

My Childhood

When our country was at peace, I could roam free and, from an early age, was full of energy. I was playing enthusiastically at kindergarten, doing somersaults over and over again by a fountain. My movements were so energetic that I lost my balance and fell on my face, cracking open my chin. There was blood everywhere. I had to be rushed to the hospital for surgery, almost giving my mother a heart attack from the shock. It looked worse than it was, but I still have a faint scar today.

Another time in kindergarten I was running so fast that, when a door was opened in front of me, I could not stop in time. I smashed into it, knocking my forehead. Blood covered my head from the injury. I nearly passed out, having to go to the hospital again for stitches. Just as it was beginning to heal, I ran into a wardrobe at kindergarten, and it fell on me, wounding the other side of my forehead. My poor teachers! I was becoming a regular at the hospital. Despite all the bumps and bruises, I never broke a bone, compared to my brothers and sisters, who all broke bones at one time or another on the ice on the roads in winter.

I didn't slow down the older I got. When I was almost seven years old, I was outside, running to jump into some water, and stepped on something sharp.

"Ahh!" I cried out, suddenly feeling the pain and falling to the ground.

It hurt so much that I didn't want anyone near my foot. Later, when a doctor came to our house to see me, I wouldn't let him touch me. I screamed whenever he came near my throbbing foot. Eventually, shrugging, he left, unable to help.

I didn't want anyone near my foot.

For three months I walked on tiptoe like a ballerina, so that the heel of my foot never touched the ground. My mother was exasperated with me, but I stubbornly refused help.

Every summer I would go and spend time with either my grandmother or aunts and uncles in other cities. That summer I went to stay with my mother's sister and her husband, the same couple who had matched my parents. They were both shocked when they saw my strange walk. Although I tried to tell them I was fine, they ignored me. Since my cousin's wife was a nurse, she was called immediately to examine my foot.

"There is something in there," she exclaimed and put some medicine in the wound to coax the object out.

It took a few days to work itself out, but eventually she was able to pull a long shard of glass out of my foot with her medical tweezers. I screamed in pain but was also stunned when I saw what had been in my flesh. It was a miracle it hadn't gotten infected, and my aunt told me I could easily have damaged my foot for life. Instead, it healed quickly. I was so relieved I no longer had to limp everywhere I went.

Visiting the Orthodox Church

During Christmas I was invited to join my Christian school friends at the Orthodox church for their celebrations. Surprisingly, Mama and Papa agreed to let me go.

"She will learn from it," Mama said to Papa.

Papa nodded. "Yes. It is important that she not be ignorant of the way others live."

My friend Munira's parents also discussed her attendance and allowed her to go with me.

Papa instructed, "Their way is not our way. Christianity is very different. You will see. Remember that as you go. Be polite, but remember who and what you are."

> "Their way is not our way. Be polite, but remember who and what you are."

With that admonition in mind, Munira and I bundled up in our warmest dress clothes and, on a very dark winter night, accompanied the Christians to the old Orthodox church. We held hands as we entered. When our Christian friends dipped their fingers in a little dish of water and made the sign of the cross, saying, "Father, Son and Holy Spirit," we exchanged uneasy glances.

I thought, *There is no god but Allah,* but did not speak.

The inside of the ancient building was illuminated with more candles than I had ever seen. The warm glow was diffused by the haze of pungent incense. Painted stars on the arched ceiling shone through the fog. There were paintings, icons and statues everywhere I looked.

I stared at a life-sized crèche near the altar. It showed baby Jesus in the manger, adored by Mary, Joseph and the shepherds. They all looked surprised as they gaped down at the baby. Jesus was not new to me. He is considered to be a prophet in the religion of Islam. I also knew that Mary was the mother of the prophet. But I wondered, *Are the figures in the scene real? Is this truly baby Jesus?* The figures did not move.

I leaned in close and asked Munira. She shook her head and whispered in my ear, "Icons."

> I stared at a life-sized crèche near the altar. I was surprised by the scene because of the strict Islamic prohibition against graven images.

My eyes widened. I was surprised by the scene because of the strict Islamic prohibition against graven images.

At that moment an organ blasted, and the congregation began to sing. A priest with a long beard and black robes entered in a procession. He sprinkled water on the congregation and, as the drops fell, the people made the sign of the cross. I felt a drop on my face and quickly wiped it away. There was more bowing and kneeling and getting up and down. Munira and I sat still in the pew. The people repeated prayers I did not understand.

Papa was right. This was very different from the mosque. I had not realized there was such a vast gulf between Islam and Christianity.

Munira whispered to me, "Unbelievers."

I agreed because everyone who is not a Muslim is considered an "infidel" in Islam.

Munira said to me quietly, "Like a show. Enjoy it. There is lots of food afterward. Cakes and sweets. Ignore the rest. This is nothing to us."

At the end of a very long service, the congregation stood to go forward and receive the bread and wine of communion—the body and blood of Jesus. I was appalled.

My Christian friend must have seen my horrified look, because she murmured, "It is only bread and wine. Don't worry."

Munira frowned. "We knew that."

I wasn't sure how Munira knew, but I was relieved to hear the news.

"You stay here," our Christian friend instructed as her family filed out past us. "We'll be back."

And so the two of us Muslims remained in the pews as the Orthodox Christians shuffled forward to receive the bread and wine—the blood and body of Jesus, a prophet of Islam. It was a very strange ritual to me.

The mass concluded, and we adjourned to a hall where giant platters of food were laid out on long tables: lamb kabobs, grilled chicken, eggs and shawarma (layers of meat, cheese and yogurt, wrapped in bread). Every kind of bread and cheese and winter vegetable was free for the taking.

Munira and I went straight for the dessert table. The golden pastry and honey-filled baklava was just like at home. I enjoyed every bite, licking honey from my fingers. *So,* I thought, *Christmas is all about candles and songs and food. A birthday celebration for one of the prophets of Islam.*

Her mouth stuffed with cake, Munira smiled. "Happy birthday, Jesus."

When we got home, Papa called me into his study. "Well?"

"Christians are very different," I reported, "and the feast was very good after."

My father seemed satisfied with his sensible daughter.

We attended other holiday celebrations, such as the Resurrection of Jesus, at the Orthodox church. Most times I did not tell my parents I was going. The feasts that followed the services made it worthwhile.

A Zealous Muslim

Since I was born a Muslim, from a young age I was determined to be good at it. I turned my attention to memorizing and reciting a set of Muslim prayers to Allah in Arabic five times a day. I was so zealous that I often prayed more than five times, kneeling on my prayer mat.

I raised my voice and shouted the first words as loudly as I could: *"Allahu akbar!"* meaning, "Allah-god is great." This was a call to prayer. Later I realized it was also a call to the war that would tear our country and our peaceful lives apart.

> **My motivation was to please Allah so I could get a ticket to heaven.**

Five evenings a week I went to Islamic classes at the Mullah's house. An old man with a long gray beard, the Mullah had many sons and two daughters, one older and the other younger than me. About eight of us girls would assemble with his daughters in their living room, and the lessons would last for an hour before sunset. Because I was trying to please Allah, I recruited friends to come with me. No one forced me to go to the lessons at the Mullah's house, but I saw my father's dedication to Islam—how he prayed five times a day and went to the mosque every Friday—and wanted to be like him. My father was my hero, and his strict observance to Islamic law inspired me.

But I was also hungry for God. My motivation was to please Allah so I could get a ticket to heaven. I was aware I was a sinner and was afraid because I knew that, if I died, I would go to hell like every Muslim.

The Mullah taught us Arabic, as well as the Qur'an, the Islamic sacred book, and *hadith*—the words, actions and stories of Muhammad. I was very zealous to know everything about Islam. I also received a foundation in the five pillars of Islam—the *shahadah* (creed), *salat* (five times a day daily prayers), *zakah* (giving to the poor), fasting during Ramadan and *hajj* (going on pilgrimage to Mecca) at least once in a lifetime. The Mullah also explained that it is important to be cleansed before prayer. My mother had already demonstrated how we were to ceremonially wash ourselves.

When boys turn twelve, they go to the mosque. It is then that they become an adult and are expected to pray and fast and live a religious life, putting their childhood behind them. We girls were not allowed in the mosque and could only go to classes with the Mullah. Women and men were always separated. It was thought that a girl became sinful at nine years old, but a boy only became sinful at twelve.

At home, our Qur'an was kept in the highest place on a shelf in my parents' bedroom, covered with a cloth. When Papa took it down, he would first ceremoniously kiss the cover, then touch his right eye with the book, kiss it again, touch the Qur'an to his left eye and kiss and finally the forehead and kiss. So much honor was shown to the book. We owned three Qur'ans, each translated into a different language.

My father would sometimes read the Qur'an to us in the evening. He never pushed it on us but read us stories when he had time. I would sit close to him, eager to absorb everything I heard. He smiled often at my keenness. I had the same hunger he had, and he approved of it.

I embraced my religion and through choice wore a veil covering my long brown hair from about the age of seven. I didn't question my beliefs and the way I was brought up. There was no reason to. I continued reciting the memorized prayers, hoping that one day Allah would answer my prayers.

But it was a monologue, not a dialogue. There was no relationship. It was beyond my wildest dreams to think I could have a relationship with God.

4

CIVIL WAR

I was ten years old when the first signs of conflict in my home city started.

I did not understand who or why great crowds gathered in the streets to march and carry banners with slogans. It was a beautiful spring day when anti-government shouts echoed in the capital and drifted in through the open windows of our apartment as we ate our evening meal.

"What are the people angry about, Papa?" I asked.

"Some people do not like our government. Other people believe we must all believe as they do and worship as they do."

Mama added, "There are men who would have us governed by Sharia Law. They would abolish the constitution, and clerics would be in charge."

"Wouldn't that be a good thing?" Adila asked. "To have the laws of Islam rule our lives?"

Papa raised his eyes, and there was some unspoken signal between him and Mama that this was not a safe topic for any of us to discuss any more. He answered, "*Insh Allah*. It will be as He wills and all will be well."

Mama said cheerfully, "It will be settled peaceably."

So the civil war began, and day by day outside the capital the conflict and killing escalated.

When the authority of the government broke down, many powerful men gathered armed militias around them and jockeyed for power. Five groups were armed with automatic weapons, explosives and hatred for their rivals. The army, the police, the Sunni militia and the Shia militia were four of the five.

The fifth group was made up of criminals we called The Mafia, who masqueraded as soldiers or rebel fighters. They took advantage of the chaos to steal, threaten, kidnap and extort money from an already terrified people.

The conflict didn't touch us, within the city, until the late summer. Then our comfortable, ordinary lives changed. Electricity only worked sporadically—on for a few hours during the day, then off until the next day.

Travel also changed. Buses stopped running because the drivers were afraid of random attacks.

Ambulances could not run, either.

I remember the day I stopped going to school in the fall. We saw a burned-out school bus still smoking, its sides riddled with bullet holes, on television.

Rumors spread quickly about which schools were closed. "There may come a day when everyone gets along—Sunni and Shia and Jews and Christian," the reporter said. "Until then, we will all hope for peace and freedom."

I went to my school to find out if it was closed. No one was there except my friend Gamila.

We sat in stunned silence. I looked at Gamila. "What do we do?"

"I guess we should go home," she answered. "Our parents will know what we should do."

We hurried home amid the *ratt-tat-tat* of distant gunfire echoing in the autumn air.

Bursting through the door, I found all my family gathered there. Mama rushed to me. "Oh, Mariam! I have been so worried about you!"

I said to Papa, "School is dismissed."

He replied, "You and your sisters will study here at home for a while."

> **We hurried home amid the ratt-tat-tat of distant gunfire echoing in the autumn air.**

I could hardly believe it. My whole life was suddenly disrupted as my eyes were opened to the religious differences that could tear personal lives apart and divide and destroy nations.

Right in My Neighborhood

Through the autumn, Air Force planes and helicopters bombed and machine-gunned enemy trucks carrying militia fighters. The aerial attacks did not discriminate between rebels and innocent families, so very soon we were all afraid to travel by car.

Abandoned vehicles lined the streets.

Sunni Muslims and Shia Muslims, brothers in our religion of Islam, fought terrible battles in the region. Much of the fighting went on just south of my home city. But worse than the skirmishes between armed squads were the atrocities committed against civilians: prominent individuals murdered; the burning of villages; genocide carried out against ethnic groups.

It was cold and overcast the day men with guns came to our neighborhood, pulling up in a truck in front of the building next to ours. I knew these men were not government soldiers but some kind of rebels or militiamen. That made them even more dangerous. All my sisters and I could do was keep still and hope they would not come for us. Adila and I ducked down, out of sight, fearful we would be shot if we were seen watching from the windows.

I heard desperate yelling coming from outside and the sounds of our neighbors begging for their lives. I could not help myself. While Adila plucked at my elbow and urged me to get down, I peered around the corner of the window frame.

The militia group had rounded up the whole family—father and two sons—and forced them into the street. "Tell us where the traitor is hiding!" we heard the rebel leader demand. "Tell us, or we'll kill you."

The militia all wore ski masks. They shouted at our neighbors and struck them repeatedly with the butts of their weapons.

"Tell us where the traitor is hiding!" we heard the rebel leader demand.

One of the rebels grabbed the younger boy by his hair and swung him around. When his father tried to intervene, another masked gunman kicked him savagely.

Suddenly one of the attackers opened fire, shooting the father in his hands and feet. It was cruelty for the sake of cruelty. As he fell to the ground, screaming in pain and pleading for mercy, the militia men laughed at him.

I gasped, my hand over my mouth, stifling a scream. My sister and I clung to each other, tears streaming down our cheeks. My heart was beating so loudly, I feared it would give us away to the gunmen. My body shook. Our neighbors were bundled into the back of a truck like sheep. Two of the attackers then jumped into the cab. The others hopped into the back with their prisoners, and the truck roared away.

We never saw those three neighbors again. All that was left of them was the blood on the asphalt and the nightmares I had for years. I realized that day that anyone with a gun had power.

There was no law; no police would come if we called; there was no one to intervene. Shia Muslims were killing Sunni Muslims and vice versa. There was no control in the country, and nobody was safe. The majority of the population in my country were Sunni Muslims, as were my family.

My family had followed the Prophet Muhammad for generations. My father was a leader in Islam. I had been searching for peace in Islam, but I now saw with my own eyes there would be no peace. Islam is a religion of war, with killing justified under the term *jihad,* which is a war or struggle against unbelievers or infidels. Yet Muslim was killing Muslim. And *jihad* exploded in my country with such horrific ethnic cleansing that many Jews and Christians were also killed.

Those who could leave the country had already fled. But my family couldn't get out. We were trapped, waiting for our fate, and I didn't know how long we would survive. Soon our local mosque closed, as it was too dangerous for people to gather together there. But we continued to pray five times a day as a family, hoping that one day Allah would stop the war.

My Father's Disappearance

Some months later a relative of ours died. In our culture it is important to show respect to the dead and to comfort the survivors. This commitment was even more important since the one who died was Jabir, meaning "Comforter," my father's uncle. Jabir had comforted and taken care of my papa, who was only five years old, as well as his youngest brother and his mom, when his father had been killed fighting as a warrior in World War II. So Papa was adamant that he should go to the funeral, despite my mother's fears for his safety.

However, he wouldn't allow any of the rest of us to accompany him. It was too dangerous, he said. "But we cannot let what

FACE to FACE with JESUS

is happening around us keep us from doing the right thing," I overheard him telling my mother. "We must stay civilized, even if the rest of the world isn't."

Jabir had lived in another city, so getting to the service would be very difficult. No buses were running, and it wasn't safe to drive in a car, but my father and some cousins decided to risk driving anyway since it would take almost a month to walk the distance.

After the first three days of Father's absence, my mother was concerned, but always tried to keep what she felt hidden from us. But I could tell she was worried. As more days passed without out his return or any word from him, I saw the strain building on her normally peaceful features. Several times I saw her staring out the window, frowning and fearful.

> "We must stay civilized, even if the rest of the world isn't."

I was worried, too—afraid that what I had seen happen to our neighbors had happened to my father. But I could never express such a thought aloud.

Then one evening, after dark, we heard the front door rattle. Because the army had imposed a curfew on our city, anyone out after sunset could be shot on sight. Mother shooed us into our bedrooms, urging, "Go! Lock the door."

Then we heard Father calling, "It's all right. It's me."

After a month away, Father had finally returned. When Adila and I hugged him, I saw he was extremely shaken. He told us he had narrowly escaped being killed.

On the third day of the journey he and his cousins had been caught in a crossfire and had to run for cover. Next they were captured by soldiers and accused of being spies, for which they could be shot.

All the cousins were interrogated separately and kept apart for many hours, with their hands and feet bound. After a day and a night, when the captors realized my father and his cousins all told exactly the same true story about the funeral, they were finally believed and released. They attended the funeral and then began the long walk back to our city.

Father was greatly alarmed at what he had experienced. As he told all of us the story, he was white as a sheet and trembling. He refused to describe the terrible sights he had seen, except to say there was much death and destruction.

My Visit to Gamila's

Battles still raged elsewhere, but the fighting in our neighborhood lessened. I was sick of being cooped up for so long and eager to get back some tiny feeling of normality in my life.

One morning, without consulting anyone, I made up my mind to visit my friend Gamila. I was old enough to take care of myself, I decided. Mother and Father had their hands full.

Since Gamila now lived in a different neighborhood, I knew I'd have to be quick as well as careful. Even as I dashed across open spaces and lingered in shadows, I enjoyed the delicious freedom of being outside. *Hey,* I thought, *there's nothing to it!* Perhaps I had been hiding when there was no longer a threat at all.

I made it to Gamila's without difficulty. She was surprised to see me but welcomed me warmly.

Sitting in the third-floor sitting room of their apartment, we chatted as if there was no war. We talked about other friends, books we enjoyed and favorite music. About an hour had passed when we heard gunfire. It was followed by squealing tires and racing engines.

By now it was second nature to drop to the floor and lie flat, safe from bullets. On hands and knees we crawled to the window overlooking the street and peeked out.

Two vehicles were driving at high speed, swerving all over the roadway, and their occupants were shooting at each other.

Suddenly the glass on the driver's side of the lead car splintered. A moment later it careened out of the street and plowed into a parked car.

The pursuing vehicle screeched to a stop alongside the wreck. Four men jumped out and started shooting into the windows of their quarry.

I had no idea who the gunmen were but instinctively knew once again that they were rebels and not government soldiers.

Four men jumped out and started shooting into the windows of their quarry.

Within moments, no one was left alive in the first car. The attackers dragged the bodies out of the wreck and dumped them on the street in a heap of bloody, lifeless corpses.

How long would they lie there? Who would pick them up? How would their families find them? My heart was breaking for the way my fellow countrymen were killing each other.

Death was very real and very close. It had exploded in my country. My family could be next.

I wondered, *How long can we survive without becoming casualties?*

FAMINE

As the war dragged on, and battles between factions increased and became more violent, things we had taken for granted became scarce. Gas and electricity were even more frequently turned off. At first we foraged for firewood from trees and shrubs. Then, desperate, we burned dry cow dung. Fuel was soon gone as everyone in the great city struggled to stay warm. We began to break up and burn the wood furniture in our house—a treasured blanket chest that was a family heirloom, our chairs and beds. Piece by piece the frigid hand of war shattered all that was comfortable and ordinary in our lives. No longer were the streets and sidewalks cleared. Heaps of dirty snow concealed frozen bodies of old and young alike.

My father and brothers did the best they could to keep us fed as the violence of the war escalated around us. They brought us potatoes, beans and sometimes apples.

Packs of wild dogs, hungry and dangerous, roamed the streets at night. I guessed that sometimes the dogs became meat for our stew pot. We did not ask where food came from when Papa or one of my brothers brought home a chunk of meat. I didn't allow myself to think of what I was eating or anticipate what the evening meal might be made of. A haunch of a horse? A wild goat or dog? An unlucky pigeon? We were merely happy to have food.

Since there was no fireplace in our apartment, Papa burned the wood outdoors, then scooped up the coals and carried them upstairs. The embers were placed into a metal bowl normally used for cooking; then the bowl was placed under a low table in the sitting room. Papa put a large blanket over the table to capture the warmth. Every member of our family slept around the table with the blanket covering us to ward off frostbite.

Our Desperate Task

It was just past noon on a snowy day in January when almost all the furniture in the apartment was gone. Papa gathered us together, preparing us for a desperate task.

"We must have fuel to keep warm, my children." He gestured at the remnants of a broken chair. "There is nothing left in the house to burn. We must find fuel today, or we will not survive. We have a few hours of daylight. There is fighting across town, but it is quiet today in our neighborhood. We will go out two by two to look for firewood. A broken branch. A plank. If you see anything that will burn, bring it home."

Mama added, "You must return before sunset. You must be indoors before the dog packs are out hunting."

"What if the soldiers come?" Adila asked.

Papa put his big hands on our shoulders. "If you hear gunfire, or a helicopter or tank approaching, hurry home. Take no chances. You must return to the apartment at the first hint of danger."

We all knew that snipers could be hiding anywhere. Our hope was that they would not set their sights on children or use us as target practice.

Mama's face was pale with worry. We dressed in our warmest clothes, then wept and clung to one another, not knowing who would make it safely back home.

Adila and I were the last two to go. Dragging a sled, as if we intended to play, we set out into the snowbound streets in search of firewood. Being the youngest, we were instructed that we must always keep the windows of our apartment building in view.

Snipers could be hiding anywhere.

"Where will we find wood?" I scanned the street and looked up at the frosty windows of our apartment. It seemed an almost hopeless task.

My sister frowned at a frozen mound. "Papa says anything will help. Look there." She pointed at the base of the snow. "Is that anything?"

Sticking out from a heap of dirty snow was the end of a single scrap of wood. We began to dig at the frozen heap with our hands in an attempt to pry it loose.

Behind me I heard the familiar voice of my friend Gamila. "Mariam! Adila!" she called as she ran toward us.

When she reached us, I noticed that her eyes were red, as though she had been crying. She looked very thin, and her cheeks were chapped with cold.

"I saw you from the window." Out of breath, she now stood beside us.

"We're trying to get wood," Adila explained.

"We broke up our chairs," Gamila said. "There is only a little left. My father says we will freeze to death." She paused. "I heard him talking to Mama about Mr. Shariq. Did you hear about him?"

Mr. Shariq, meaning "Compassionate," was a Shia Muslim who taught my favorite subject in school, math. He was a patient and kind man, filled with compassion for students who struggled with the concepts of mathematics. He was also a principal assistant, the vice president of the school.

We were Sunni Muslims, and though there was enormous conflict between our denomination and the Shia Muslims, my family continued to be at peace with people of all beliefs.

I straightened and searched her face. "I have not seen him since they closed the school. He is Shia, Papa says, so it is very unsafe for him on our side of the neighborhood."

Gamila nodded sadly. "He's dead."

Adila gasped. "Dead! Not Mr. Shariq!"

I cried, "He can't be dead. No!" My thoughts turned to the kindhearted math teacher.

At that instant the sound of a helicopter chopped at the air. We dashed toward the entrance of our building and rushed inside.

"Tell us what happened! Are you sure he's dead, Gamila?"

Gamila spilled the details. "They came for him. The militia. I don't know if it was Sunni or Shia. Does it matter anymore? They are all animals. They beat him in front of his wife and children. Dragged him away. He was missing for days, and then someone said his body washed up on the bank of the river." She choked out the final details. "He was barefoot."

Adila began to cry.

"Oh no!" I sobbed.

Gamila bit her lip. "No one knows. They are all killing each other, and no one even remembers why or what the war is about. But the facts are, they tortured him and he's dead, all right."

Weeping, we three girls climbed the stairs to our apartments. I was no longer hungry. I didn't feel the cold. I was numb. I grieved deeply for Mr. Shariq, who had been like a kind uncle to me. He was an inspirational teacher and made me love mathematics.

Now, however, when I thought of the subject, a sick feeling came to my stomach as I imagined my teacher's lifeless form floating in the water, the light gone from his eyes, blood drained from his body. I would have nightmares as I tried to sleep at night, but the sound of bombs and bullets ensured my sleep was never deep, and I often awakened with a start at the noise of an explosion nearby.

Through wracking sobs, we told my mother the news about Mr. Shariq. What would become of his wife and children? But we knew that we could not help. In this civil war, they were Shia, and we were Sunni. Suddenly the gulf between us was a valley of death.

They were Shia, and we were Sunni. Suddenly the gulf between us was a valley of death.

One by one, my brothers and sisters returned with their arms heaped with scrap wood. There were tears of relief from us at their return. Mama told Papa about Mr. Shariq and that she no longer wanted us girls to go out on the street.

Papa put his hands on my shoulders. "I know you are very sad, Mariam. There is nothing to be done. Nothing at all. Senseless, brutal violence."

Papa then straightened up. He gave Mama a directive. "We must all dress in the drabbest clothes we own. The girls must cover themselves completely from now on. No one is safe."

Mama nodded. "All right, then. Yes. I agree. From now on, no color on our clothing to draw attention or even a stitch of embroidery outside this apartment."

That night Papa brought the coals up and put them in the metal bowl. We covered ourselves with the blanket draped over the table and all lay like the spokes of a wheel with our heads pointed in toward the warmth.

Papa whispered to Mama, "I do not know how to keep my daughters safe from such madness. There is no law in our country—only hunger, cold and vengeance."

Mr. Shariq's murder was my introduction to death as a child, and very soon I was to see and hear much worse. My innocence and childhood were irrevocably stolen. Life was now about survival, and we had to fight for it.

Rumors of Food

Food became increasingly scarce. In my prayers to Allah I asked again and again for us to be fed and warm.

Allah did not answer my prayers. Shia Muslims continued to kill Sunni Muslims, and vice versa. Radicals cried for the death of democracy and a return to Sharia Law. I continued to ask Allah for help, but no help came.

When we heard rumors of food, others heard those rumors, too, creating long lines and presenting snipers with opportunities to strike. There was only one place in the city where bread was baked and distributed by the government. The official ration was one loaf of bread per person. Thousands flocked to the gates to wait in breadlines for hours to receive a ration.

Allah did not answer my prayers.

Mama and two of my sisters were ill and would not survive the journey and the cold. It was up to the rest of us to bring home enough to share.

Before dawn, despite the danger and the freezing cold, we made our tearful farewells and trudged with Papa toward the bread factory. Snow crunched beneath our feet like the sound of gunshots.

Adila's breath rose in the cold like puffs of steam. "I am so cold, Mariam!" Her teeth chattered as we took our places at the back of a serpentine line swelled with thousands of starving citizens.

"Pretend you're someplace warm." I clung to her. "Pretend we're on a tropical, warm island, where there is always summer and sunshine!" I laughed, and we jumped up and down to keep our feet from freezing.

Slowly the dawn broke and the line crept forward. Soldiers with automatic weapons patrolled the line to keep order. We leaned against one another to rest. Mid-morning we inched past the frozen bodies of an elderly couple who had not survived the night.

"They sat down to rest," said a young woman behind us as we stared at them. "You can't sit down. You can't sleep. This is what happens."

My father called to a soldier, "You should take these bodies away."

The soldier shrugged. "They aren't hurting anyone."

Papa stood between us and our view of the dead. He tried to keep our thoughts occupied with memories of warm summer days on my grandparents' farm in the country. "What was your favorite part of summer?" he asked.

I considered my answer carefully. "Warm sun on my back beside the lake? Riding horses? Helping gather eggs from the hens?"

Adila blurted, "Breakfast. And lunch. And dinner."

We laughed, but the truth was that present hunger gnawing at our stomachs had made every happy memory center around food.

Ahead of us, a young woman with a baby in her arms started to wail. "My baby! My baby! Someone help me! Oh please! Please!"

Others gathered around her as her screams grew louder. An officer shouldered through. Moments passed and the word came back to us: "The baby is dead."

"Froze to death."

"It was sick anyway."

Armed men in heavy coats led the weeping mother away.

"Why did she bring it out in the cold?"

"Poor woman. But why would she bring a sick child to the breadline?"

Adila and I exchanged glances. We knew why. The choice was freezing to death or dying at home of starvation.

The sun set, and it grew very dark. A frigid wind blew down from the mountains. Snow flurries stung our cheeks. Would we ever reach the front gates of the factory? Those who were too weak to carry on sat on the heaps of snow. Some died right there.

Adila whispered hoarsely, "We can't sit down. We can't sleep until we get our ration and get home to Mama."

I nodded and closed my eyes against the cold.

The crowd became restless as the rumor spread there would not be enough for us.

"What's taking so long?" someone complained loudly. "Can't they see we are freezing to death?"

"They've run out of bread," wailed another.

"They have no more bread to give us!" a man shouted.

Others joined in the clamor. Suddenly the shouts became demanding. Violence broke out as the starving mob pushed at the gates.

Soldiers fired into the air, but the panic increased.

Violence broke out as the starving mob pushed at the gates.

Papa tried to shield us as the pushing became a crush. "Stay close to me!"

Bullets whizzed past my head. Adila ordered, "Hold on to my hand. Don't let go!"

Blood sprayed the snow as someone next to me was hit. Then two more fell as stray bullets crashed into them.

Terrified shrieks increased until I could hardly hear my father's voice.

Suddenly Adila let go of my hand. "Mariam, stay with Papa. I'm going!" she cried above the din.

"Going where?"

"I've got to try to get us bread!"

"You can't. They'll kill you!"

"We will die here if I don't go. I love you!"

"Please, Adila, don't . . ."

"I will come back."

The shoving and violence all around me tore my sister from me.

Papa braced himself, protecting me from being crushed to death. "Where is Adila?"

"She's gone! She said she would try to get bread!"

I heard Papa call her name, but it was too late. We were caught up in the swarming mob as bullets tore through the crowd.

A woman beside me was killed by a gunfire burst. I was knocked to the ground beside her. Papa, through superhuman strength, kept me from being trampled and crushed to death.

The riot ended. Too many had died. The soldiers demanded that we all must disperse or be shot. Over twenty hours of waiting and we had nothing to show for it.

Papa held me tightly as we picked our way out of the chaos. "Mariam, we must find your sister."

I sobbed, "Adila, where are you? Adila!"

Papa and I stood panting in the dark, shouting Adila's name.

A soldier shoved Papa with the butt of his gun. "Get out of here! Everyone must go now."

"But my daughter . . . I must find my twelve-year-old daughter."

In that instant, Adila was at my elbow. "Here I am, Papa." Her eyes were wide. "Come. Hurry. We must go!"

Papa wept with relief. "Where did you go? If something had happened, your mother would not have forgiven me. Adila, where did you go?"

She did not answer. The soldier turned away. Plucking at Papa's sleeve, Adila led us some distance from the crowd.

She paused before swinging a bag out from under her coat. "It's still warm," she whispered.

"What?" Papa gasped.

"Yes. Still warm. Hurry, Papa. There will be enough to share."

We wound our way through the dark streets toward home. The burlap bag filled with 36 loaves of bread was worth more than sacks of gold.

> **Through the courage of my sister we had enough to share with our neighbors and rations that lasted us almost a week.**

We could hardly breathe as we hurried past knots of people talking about the bread riots and the many who had died that night.

We did not dare to speak until we entered our apartment and slumped onto the floor. Through the courage of my sister we had enough to share with our neighbors and rations that lasted us almost a week.

Adila's Courage

Once we were home, Adila told us her story.

She had fearlessly dashed toward the high fence that protected the factory from the outside. As the riots continued at her back, she scaled the wire, throwing herself over the top. Then she raced wildly toward the second fence as the clatter of bullets seemed to pursue her.

Without a moment's hesitation she clambered over the second fence, cutting herself on concertina wire at the top. She expected the searing pain of a bullet in her back, but the scent of baking bread drove her on. Flashes of gunfire illuminated the night as the guards and soldiers flocked to defend against the starving mob. Inside the usually closely guarded grounds there were no soldiers in sight. They were all in defensive positions at the gates.

Adila sneaked close to the building. The scent of fresh bread beckoned her toward a window. There was a fraction of an inch opening, and she managed to pry it wider apart.

Suddenly she was in the bakery! Warm ovens heated the air. Heaps of warm bread were piled on the racks. She searched for something to carry the bounty away. A single burlap bag lay crumpled on the floor.

Adila opened it and scooped loaves into the sack—one dozen, then two dozen, then another dozen loaves. She scanned the floor, praying for another bag, but did not find one.

The next minute the harsh voices of soldiers and bakery workers sounded at the front of the building. They were returning to their posts.

Adila ducked down and, dragging the sack of bread behind her, hurried to the open window. With effort, she slung her bounty out onto the snowy ground then scrambled out after it. Closing the window, she hefted the sack and began her journey back to us.

For Adila, that was only the beginning. She grew more courageous as the war continued. She now knew how and where to get bread. Without telling anyone but me, she risked her life for us all.

Two weeks later, a tank, surrounded by a small squad of soldiers, clanked past below our windows.

Adila watched it go. As soon as it turned the corner at the end of the block she said, "I'm going now."

"Wait! I'm coming, too," I said, even though I was small for my age and weak from lack of food.

Adila shook her head. "Absolutely not. You'd only slow me down." Holding my hands in both of hers, she bent to look me in the eye. We both knew the risks she was taking: if she was caught alone, she would be raped and then killed.

Since she would be approaching from the rear of the plant, she would have to scale the fence to enter the grounds after dashing down narrow streets and hiding whenever anyone else appeared.

From our window I watched her emerge from our building, hiding briefly beside an abandoned car. Then she darted across the street, into an alley and out of sight.

Adila was a fast runner and confident. What was taking her so long?

When Adila had been away for an hour, it already seemed like days. I was concerned. How long could it take? Adila was a fast runner and confident. What was taking her so long?

She finally reemerged from the alley with a big bag full of loaves of bread. Pausing to look around carefully before coming out of the safety of the alley, I saw her glance up at our window. Nodding toward me, even though she could not see me, she raised the sack proudly. "Look what I found," the gesture said.

She was at the entry to the alley where the brick walls of the building opposite ours formed a corner.

A bullet struck just above Adila's head, showering her hair with dark red dust. The sound of the sniper's firing came a second later, but Adila was already racing across the street.

When the second shot came, slamming into the wall of our building, she was already back inside the doorway and safe.

Once in our home I hugged her and cried that she had almost been killed. There were torn places in her sweater from climbing over a chain-link fence and squeezing through a narrow passage.

"Don't ever do that again!" I urged.

Adila shrugged. "We have to eat."

We both knew that, before the war ended, there would be many more times when great courage and cunning would be required.

During that time, we learned to live on our knees. It was no longer safe to stand up in our apartment. We crawled from room to room, below the level of the windows, lest we be targeted and shot.

One afternoon a burst of shooting erupted outside our apartment.

Adila warned, "Snipers in the building across the street!"

But Mama remained frozen in terror as an infrared sniper laser targeted her heart.

"Mama, move!" I yelled.

The instant she dropped to her knees, the sniper pulled the trigger. The bullet buzzed right past her head. My sisters and I crawled to where she lay on the floor. I could see the bullet hole in the wall where she had been standing. A fraction of a second later and she would have died.

> **The instant she dropped to her knees, the sniper pulled the trigger.**

I wept and held her close, praying for the nightmare to end.

But the fighting only grew worse. It was as if we were living in a nightmare—a horror movie that did not end.

The whir of the helicopter and the drone of a plane sent us scrambling for cover in the basement as bombs began to fall.

Why were Muslims killing Muslims? Where was Allah when we prayed to him?

Worth the Risk?

Winter crept in, and we were firmly locked in the second year of war. Adila and I heard that a bakery might be getting a fresh supply of bread.

"We should go," Adila said firmly. "We should try to get a ration."

That afternoon we decided it was worth the risk to our safety. Bundled up with coats and hats, we hurried along the deserted streets in biting cold and gathered with hundreds of others to wait for the shop to open.

The streets were blanketed with snow. We stamped our feet in an attempt to stay warm as we waited in line.

Darkness fell. We could not leave our place in line, so we crouched together in the snow and attempted to sleep. Tucking our faces close to one another, we prayed that morning would come soon.

An elderly man and two elderly women froze to death through that long night. Adila and I were both blue with cold. I could not feel my hands or feet as dawn crept over the tops of the buildings.

Snow glistened in the soft morning light. Voices stirred the morning air as crowds of new arrivals flooded the street.

They had not been waiting in line as we had. They knew they would not get any bread because they had come too late. In desperation, the crowd swelled and surged forward toward the bakery. Men and women climbed over those who had been waiting in the snow. I was caught unaware by a boot crashing onto my head.

I screamed in shock, "Help!" I tried to scramble up out of danger. Somehow Adila and I were separated, and I was trapped between two large people. My cheek was crushed against someone's back. My breath was being squeezed out of me.

I felt consciousness slipping away. Just at that moment, the police arrived and fired their guns in the air, causing the mob to retreat. The bodies crushing me released just enough for me to draw a breath and escape from the press.

Even though I was no longer being crushed, the police were now firing at the people. Many of those who had been waiting

Famine

all night for bread were killed or trampled and badly injured. I was terrified! Bullets sprayed the air, missing me by fractions.

I had been crying out to Allah and Muhammad, praying my set Arabic prayers, but there was no answer. Losing all hope, I cried out in desperation to the God of Abram, Isaac and Jacob in my own language. I knew He was the God of Christians and Jews, and I wondered if He would somehow be able to help me.

"Creator God, if You exist and if You are real, please help me!" I cried, knowing it would be a miracle if I survived.

I screamed in shock, "Help!" I tried to scramble up out of danger.

Suddenly a supernatural calm and relief descended upon me, as if an angel pulled me out of the chaos.

An instant later my sister Adila was in front of me. Her arms were full of bread. "Quick! Let's get out of here!" she called then began to run.

I followed with all the strength I had left.

We didn't slow down until we got home. I was panting and out of breath when we arrived at our apartment. Papa had also just returned from trying to find bread.

We told him what had happened.

"My daughters! I wish I had been there to protect you!"

Papa hugged us close, tears in his eyes. He was deeply shaken by how close we had come to dying.

That night, as I tried to sleep, I pondered what had happened. The God of Abram, Isaac and Jacob had answered my prayers. Did that mean He was alive?

71

6

THE HOLY BOOK

During the upheaval and terror of the civil war, many young women were raped and murdered. Sometimes their bodies were left as warnings for everyone to see. Sometimes they were thrown into the river.

A close friend of mine from school was taken off the street by soldiers when she was only thirteen. She was left to die after the attack but somehow found the strength to make her way home. She was both physically and emotionally brutalized by what had happened, and shock waves skittered through our community.

We all knew there would be no justice for the crime. This was war, and our city had become more lawless than a jungle.

My family realized they could not be with us girls at all times. As my sisters and I went into the streets to find food, we were very vulnerable to attack.

Father and Mother were particularly worried about me as I was the smallest. Because I was weak, I would not be able to defend myself against any sort of assault.

In the end it was my brother Musa who came up with the solution. He discussed it with Papa, and they told me of their plan. "A friend of mine is giving karate lessons. I think you should take them," Musa said.

My eyes lit up! I loved sports, and the lessons would be a welcome relief from the fearful monotony of life. I was a natural athlete, despite being small and often sick with colds and headaches as a child. Before the war I had taken Kung Fu classes and had excelled. My coach had even spoken of taking me to Asia to train professionally. My parents did not allow me to go, saying I was too young to make such a journey. I had also played for my school in volleyball and basketball and had trained as a gymnast. A friend's father worked at the circus, and he taught me and his daughter. His training enabled me to become very fit and flexible.

There was one problem with me starting the karate class: lack of money. With the start of the civil war there had been an economic crash in my country. Our currency became worthless and, as a result, my father went bankrupt, losing all his money in one day. He had been a very rich man and once told us that he had enough to buy sixteen houses, but it was all gone.

My father went bankrupt, losing all his money in one day.

The shock caused him to have heart pains so severe that the doctors thought he would have a heart attack. Mercifully he didn't, but his decline in financial circumstances affected him deeply, and he was depressed for a long time. The inheritance he had worked all his life to give to his children was gone in a moment. My father was not alone in his bankruptcy; many of our friends and family lost everything, too.

In our culture it is expected that the father will buy each of his sons a house when that son marries, while giving each of his daughters a dowry. Before losing everything, Papa had been so focused on the future, building up his fortune to provide for his sons and daughters, that he forgot to live each day at a time. During the war, he couldn't continue being a lawyer and philosophy professor. Instead he tried to find any job to bring some income into the home. He embraced the time with family more because he realized we were his true riches.

Because Papa had no money, he could not send me to karate. But my brother Musa offered to pay for the classes since, although his business had also crashed, he was being paid by the army.

Drawn to Jesus

Three days a week I made the short five-minute journey to my old school gym where the karate lessons were being held. The classes were for everyone. There were about fifty of us—men, women and children—and I took to it like a duck to water.

The training and being together with friends was pleasant relief in such hard times . . . an outlet from the stresses and tensions of war. Most of us in the class were Muslim, and we'd often talk about Allah when the class was over. There was a hunger among the people to know more, so we started to discuss the *hadith*, wanting to learn how to be better Muslims.

I think it was because of our spiritual eagerness that, at the end of one of the classes, our Muslim karate instructor mentioned he had a children's Bible. "Here it is. It's like the Qur'an," he said, handing me a beautifully illustrated hardback Bible. He added that many stories in the Qur'an were also in the Bible, and this sparked my interest. I turned over the pages and was immediately attracted by the artwork. It was so different from the Qur'an, which has no illustrations.

74

Although our instructor was a Muslim by birth, he was not practicing Islam. He made no secret of the fact that he was searching spiritually, and I assume that is why he had a Bible. However I was still shocked when he so openly told the class about it. I knew the Bible was the holy book of Christians, and they were the infidel. *Kafir* was the term we used, usually translated as "unbeliever" or "disbeliever" or sometimes "infidel." However, I also knew the Bible contained stories about the God of Abraham, Isaac and Jacob, and I wanted to know more about Him.

My friend and neighbor Rashida, meaning "Rightly Guided," who came to the karate classes with me, was as curious as I was to see what the Bible said. She had a worn and tattered New Testament with illustrations in her home. She would smuggle it out of the house so we could read it in the street.

I was amazed to learn about Jesus healing and even raising the dead. I was touched by His miracles, as I knew that Muhammad had not performed any.

"Don't let anyone see," she warned me. "I will be in trouble if my family finds out."

I was amazed to learn about Jesus healing and even raising the dead. I was touched by His miracles, as I knew that Muhammad had not performed any.

I began to dream of one day owning a Bible for myself.

After I started to read the children's Bible, Jesus appeared to me in dreams, showing me that He is the only way to follow (John 14:6). I saw Him as a Middle Eastern–looking man in a white robe, with a very bright light shining out from Him. I can't remember Him ever speaking to me in those dreams, but I would wake up with a deep sense of peace. My heart was being gently drawn to Jesus. During the intervals when we had electricity at home I flicked through the TV channels and came across American cartoons called the "Super Book—Living Book," translated into my language. They were about Jesus and His miracles and very quickly became my favorite programs. I would sit glued to the TV, watching the cartoon Gospel stories. I couldn't get over the signs and wonders of Jesus.

Besides the influence of the cartoons and my karate teacher's Bible, something else brought an awareness of Jesus into my life. When I was thirteen, the *Jesus* film came to our neighborhood. We heard an announcement that a film was going to be shown in the street below. We were still in the middle of the war, but after three years of killing, people were so tired of fear and oppression that they were willing to risk their lives for a bit of light relief.

We hadn't been able to go to the cinema because of the war, so the film was a big deal for all of our neighbors. Nearly two hundred people attended, sitting on mats and chairs in the street in the early evening before it got dark. It was a big event, a celebration, and everyone was spellbound watching the story of Jesus of Nazareth. We loved watching Him become a carpenter and then perform many miracles with His disciples.

When I saw Jesus hanging on the cross, I could not stop crying. My family and friends were crying, too, because all of us had been touched by the story.

After seeing the film, I realized that there was much more to Jesus than I had thought. I had so many questions that I went to talk to my father.

"Papa, Jesus is the only prophet I know who made the blind see, healed the sick, made the deaf hear and the paralyzed walk. He can't only be a prophet; He must be more. Jesus not only raised the dead; He was also raised from the dead Himself. His tomb is empty. He is alive. Muhammad's bones are still buried in Mecca, and he is dead. Jesus is my Superhero!" I said to my father.

Father sat back in his chair and smiled at me. "Yes, Jesus was one of the greatest prophets, even in Islam. We know in the end times He will come from heaven as a judge to judge the world," he replied.

When Papa told me Jesus would come again to judge the world, he unknowingly inspired me to learn more about Him. He was a prophet, but was He more than that? I wondered. I determined in my heart to search out an answer that would satisfy me. The miracles of Jesus had captured me, and I would not walk away until I knew for sure who He was.

"Jesus is my Superhero!" I said to my father.

My father was not angry that I had been looking at the Bible. He had read it himself, being a well-educated man. He approved of my inquiring mind.

Had he known my searching would lead me to leave Islam, he would have forced me to stop right then.

7

TREMENDOUS REVELATIONS

It was my friend Munira who brought me the news about a new martial arts class being offered near my home.

"Have you seen this?" she asked excitedly, waving a poster yanked from a telephone pole in my face.

"What? Stop," I said, pushing her back, while at the same time grabbing the flyer out of her hand. "Tae kwon do," I read. "Self-defense training. Beginners welcome."

The civil war had already been going on for several years. Every day brought new reports of women and young girls being seized off the streets, raped and often murdered.

Mastering self-defense was already a powerful desire of mine. It was not only a skill I wanted in order to protect myself, but so I could use it to rescue others. As captain of several sports teams in school, I had always hated all forms of bullying.

For three years I had received instruction in kung fu, kickboxing and then karate. I had even progressed to the point of training beginners in karate myself. But as the economy worsened and our family finances tightened, my brother Musa, who had been paying my tuition, told me I had to give up karate.

"So?" I replied to Munira. "I still can't afford it."

"Read on," Munira returned triumphantly. "It's free!"

"Free?" It was music to my ears! The flyer went on to state that the instruction was without cost and was being held in the gymnasium of the local school. All participants had to provide was their own workout clothing.

"How can they do this for free? Maybe it means the first lesson is free and then they charge."

"No," Munira said triumphantly. "See: 'Never a charge. Everyone welcome.' But I don't know the real reason they can do it for free."

I spoke with my karate instructor about the new program. He had always treated me like a little sister and was sorry I had to drop out of his class. He wanted me to continue some form of training. "I have also heard of this tae kwon do instruction," he said. "By all means, try it. If you like it, then it will be good for you, I'm sure."

To my delight my parents agreed that keeping up with my training was a good idea. They supported my decision to join the new class and encouraged me to take the practices and exercises seriously.

A God of "Love" and a "Father"

On the first day of the new program, Alim (meaning "Learned, expert, scholar"), the tae kwon do coach, introduced himself and said, "Please, everyone sit down."

We complied. There were no workout mats, so we sat on the scraped and scarred wooden floor of the gym.

He then asked for and wrote down all of our names. There were 45 students in the class—a mixture of boys and girls from age fourteen to late twenties and even early thirties. Because my country had been under Communist rule, there was no enforced restriction against men and women going to class together.

There were 45 of us in the beginning class and only one coach and one assistant coach. From its Korean origin, the name of the sport roughly means "the way of the foot and the hand." Combining kicks, punches, strikes, sweeps, throws and blocking maneuvers, tae kwon do uses rapid blows and high leg movements to disable an attacker. As a sport it trains an athlete in agility and balance and in the concentration of mental and physical power.

"For those of you who are new to the sport, tae kwon do is a discipline of the mind and spirit, as well as of the body," Alim explained. "It is important to develop both. And since the spirit is more powerful than the body, we will always begin our session by exercising it first. Now repeat after me: "I can do all things. . . .""

"I can do all things," we dutifully repeated.

The experienced students called out the words with enthusiasm, while Munira and I mumbled them.

"I can do all things through Christ, who strengthens me."

"Christ?" I whispered to Munira. "Like Jesus Christ? Like Christian?"

Munira shushed me. "He's with the Americans, and they're all Christians. It doesn't mean anything."

But I was shocked. We were in a Muslim country, yet Alim, who was a European, openly and boldly spoke about Jesus Christ. I knew he could be persecuted for speaking out as he did. At the same time, I was intrigued.

When he talked about Jesus Christ as "the God of love," I was even more startled. In Islam, there are 99 names of Allah, but none of them are Love. All my life I had been taught that Allah was distant and a strict judge. If I sinned, he would punish me.

I was in constant fear of him because I knew I was a sinner and that sin separated me from a relationship with him.

I had done everything I could to please him with my prayers, my fasting, my good deeds and all the rest, but I had no peace. No matter how much I did, or how hard I tried, I knew in my own heart I could not possibly be enough. I was too often unable to measure up.

Alim spoke of a God who was not distant and disapproving—a God who wanted a personal relationship with us. Then he said that God knew my name!

I shivered with the thought.

No matter how much I did, or how hard I tried, I knew in my own heart I could not possibly be enough.

"I didn't know any of your names before you came to class today," Alim said. "But long before that, even before any of you were born, God knew your names. He has a plan for your lives. He created each of you in His image. That's what the Bible says in Genesis 1:27 (NIV): 'So God created mankind in his own image, in the image of God he created them; male and female he created them.'"

Once more, I was startled.

In Islam it would be regarded as blasphemous to think we were created in Allah's image. "Allah has no offspring," we are taught. Out of the 99 names for Allah in Islam another name missed is that of "Father." That's because Muslims are descendants of Ishmael, the son of Abraham, who was rejected by his father and then sent out with his mom, Hagar, to the wilderness. Ishmael then became an orphan. That is why Muslims believe Jesus cannot be the Son of God, because the god of Islam—Allah—has no children and is not a father.

It was also amazing to think that the God of whom Alim spoke had a plan for my life. He quoted Psalm 139:13–14 (NIV):

For you created my inmost being; you knit me together in my mother's womb. I praise you because I am fearfully and wonderfully made; your works are wonderful, I know that full well.

This verse drove deep into my heart as I realized I was known to God even before I was born and that He made me wonderfully. In Islam, a woman is second class and has no rights, no voice and no value. For the first time in my life I dared to believe that I was of real value to God. It was thrilling to have value as a woman.

> **A shaft of light beamed into my heart, enabling me to believe that hope was possible.**

The next verses he shared were Isaiah 43:1 and 49:16: "I have called you by name; you are Mine!" and "See, I have engraved you on the palms of my hands" (NIV).

My head was spinning as the revelation of a God who regarded me as valuable impacted my soul. Out of six billion humans on the planet, God knew me and chose me and called me by name!

Alim then quoted Luke 12:7: "The very hairs on your head are all numbered."

What? This Christian God really must value me if He knows how many hairs there are on my head. I don't even know how many there are, I thought. Could He really value me that much?

Finally Alim mentioned Jeremiah 29:11: "'For I know the plans I have for you,' declares the LORD, 'plans to prosper you and not to harm you, plans to give you hope and a future'" (NIV).

I had been marked by hopelessness over the past years, and now a shaft of light beamed into my heart, enabling me to believe that hope was possible.

My heart was warmed by those thoughts, as nothing before in my life had ever moved me. But I still had so many questions.

Alim also told us how Jesus spoke up for the oppressed and

the outcasts of His society. "What you will learn in our training is always to be used to defend and protect those who need it most."

Then he went on to tell us about the rules and expectations of the class. He said the normally two-hour sessions would stretch to more than three hours on weekdays, since we would spend time singing worship songs, praying and studying the Bible. He also invited us to attend church on Sunday with him, saying that, for the Christian, Sunday is the holy day like Friday is for the Muslims.

I accepted the right of a teacher to maintain the atmosphere in his own classroom and to instruct according to his training regimen. *Besides,* I thought, *this is a humble man who is offering to teach us for free. Who am I to argue?*

Finally, Alim prayed for us—that we would benefit from the training, that we and our families would be safe from harm, that our country would be delivered from the war and that our hearts would be open to the leading of the Lord.

Almost against my will, I felt another thrill at his words. They had gone straight to my inner longing for a way to reach God.

After that, I asked Hakim (meaning "Wise"), another coach, if he believed that Jesus was God's Son.

Hakim understood the Muslim way of thinking. He could not come right out and assert, "Jesus is the Son of God, and you must believe it." If he had spoken like that, my mental and emotional shutters would have come down. I would not have been able to listen to anything else he said, much less accept the idea of Jesus as Lord. For a Muslim, Allah is so holy that to suggest he has a son is inconceivable and blasphemy.

So when I asked Hakim, "Is Jesus God's Son?" he simply handed me a thin paperback copy of the gospel of John. "Read this, and it will give you the answers you are looking for."

I started reading the book immediately. The light of God's truth crept slowly, bit by bit, step by step, into my heart. As John 3:16 says, "For God so loved the world that He gave His one and only Son, that whoever believes in Him shall not perish but have eternal life" (NIV).

I had no idea at that time the words would lead to a life-changing revelation and a relationship with the one true God.

8

ENCOUNTER WITH LOVE

I cried out to Allah faithfully five times a day, every day, but he never answered even one prayer. I prayed for food, and we were hungry. I prayed for peace, and the war became more violent.

Gamila and I were both fourteen. We often talked about what life was like outside our broken, violent country. I dreamed of a world without death and war where people were not killed for what they believed. Freedom and democracy, once the hope of my nation, had been forgotten in the years of civil war.

Alim invited all of us who were taking free tae kwon do instruction to come to church the following Sunday. I agreed to go. My friend Gamila, who had also started tae kwon do, decided to come with me. We had attended the same school and done everything together since kindergarten.

We both knew that attending a Christian service was a dangerous step to take. Muslims were being tortured and killed for less. If my family and community found out, I would be branded a traitor to my Muslim faith. I understood what it meant for me as a Muslim to go into a Christian place of worship. Muslims believe that our religious destiny is assigned by birth. Islam is our identity. It is not a matter of choice. Rejecting or changing my religious heritage would make me an infidel. Therefore my decision to go to church with my coach might cost me my life.

I knew if I died, I would go to hell, yet the world I lived in seemed like hell. I was constantly bombarded with fear and death.

I was constantly bombarded with fear and death.

I had no relationship with Allah. None of my prayers had been answered. I did, however, have questions about Jesus and the God of Abraham, Isaac and Jacob. But I could never admit to my mother, father or brothers that I intended to go to church.

"I will be attending another training event," I told them and didn't explain further that it was spiritual training.

"I am so happy you are learning to defend yourself," Papa answered as I put on my coat and prepared to leave.

He would have been devastated if he had known what I was really doing that cold fall Sunday in the mid 1990s when I left my home on a journey that would change my life forever.

Welcomed by Love and Joy

I waved at Gamila waiting beside the school building. Peering over my shoulder, I wondered if anyone was watching us. Was it possible someone could see by my expression that I was about to do something dangerous?

I shrugged away the worry. "I told them you and I were going to a training event. You?"

"The same. They didn't ask about details."

"It takes an hour to walk to the church," I said, "so we better

get going." Our cheeks were rosy with the cold and our breath
hung in the air as we talked.

We were to meet Alim at a location nearby, then follow him
to the church.

"Alim had better hurry or we'll be late."

Minutes passed before Alim arrived on his bicycle, his big
German shepherd right behind him. "I'm glad you came. I wasn't
sure you would show up. Let's go."

We followed him closely, our bodies warming as we walked
quickly. I was nervous and excited at the same time, as well as
very curious about what to expect.

It took us an hour to reach the
building. I hesitated before entering as I remembered the Orthodox church I'd visited. But as we
stepped in, the atmosphere was completely different. We were
welcomed at the door by smiling young people who called out
greetings:

> **The feeling of love permeated everything.**

"We are so happy you are here!"

"Jesus loves you!"

"Glad you came!"

I was amazed.

The feeling of love permeated everything—the kind of love
Jesus talks about:

> "A new command I give you: Love one another. As I have loved
> you, so you must love one another. By this everyone will know
> that you are my disciples, if you love one another."
>
> John 13:34–35 NIV

I witnessed the full meaning of that command that morning.
I wanted what they had. I knew something was missing in my
life. I was not joyful. I was not satisfied.

Gamila and I locked arms as we were escorted to our seats. We were both in awe. Growing up we had heard so much negative propaganda about Christians and the church. This was far different from my early experience in the Orthodox church. Instead of hundreds of candles lighting the room, the light came from within the Christians who greeted one another and who welcomed us. I was impressed by their joy. How I longed for that kind of joy. I had lived with such hopeless depression through the war because of the fighting and brutality. Now all around me were ordinary people, just like me, who had suffered the same things I had suffered and perhaps more. Yet they were able to rejoice. I was fascinated!

Gamila and I sat at the back in the pews, hoping no one would notice us. The building was packed, with about eight hundred to a thousand people. The offering basket came around. It had a cross on it, the sign of the infidel. I was convinced it would make me unclean if I touched it, so I didn't.

The pastor was an American in his fifties. His expression was full of love. He had come to my country with the tae kwon do coach when God had asked them to preach the Good News of peace to the Muslim nations of the Middle East.

The worship in the church was conducted in a European language that was understood by all the different ethnic groups. Songs were projected onto a screen so we could see and read the words.

As the congregation worshiped Jesus, I looked around in wonder. This was not a religion. This was a relationship with the Creator! People from many different nations, young and old, were all unified by God's love as they sang beautiful worship songs.

I found the huge cross on stage terrifying and tried not to look at it. To a Muslim, the cross where Jesus was crucified was an instrument of torture and death for criminals. It made me think, *Death is following me even here.*

After the songs were finished, the pastor stood and searched the audience with his gaze. "Are there any visitors or newcomers among us?"

Gamila looked at me. "Don't stand up," she whispered.

We were conspicuous in our Muslim head scarves and we knew it, so we slouched lower in our seats. But we were recognized as new and thus were encouraged to stand. Feeling uncomfortable and awkward, we stood as the people applauded and sang to us, "We greet you in the name of Jesus Christ! He loves you and we love you! So we greet you in the name of Jesus Christ."

Color climbed to my cheeks, warming them, and I smiled shyly. The sense of joy surrounding us helped us relax as we both sat down, feeling loved by the congregation.

Gamila leaned close to me. "This is very nice."

I nodded. "I'm glad we came."

The guest speaker was a woman from America who spoke with the help of a translator. She was filled with a heavenly power I had never seen in anyone before. Like Moses in Exodus (24:18; 34:28), she had fasted forty days and forty nights, drinking only water, before she came to preach.

I leaned closer. Now I heard something new: "Jesus was sent into this world to live a perfect life and die for our sins. He is the final sacrifice for your sins and mine. He died on the cross, was buried, and on the third day rose from the dead! To all who call on His name, He promises forgiveness and mercy and eternal life!"

This was indeed profound. I considered her words carefully. But I also needed a sign and a wonder to prove it was true.

Then the invitation came. "If you would like to be forgiven and have eternal life, you can do that right now by asking Jesus into your heart. Come forward and we will pray with you."

Gamila and I looked at one another with expressions that cried, "NO!"

There was no way we would ask Jesus into our hearts, no matter how deeply her words touched us.

Then, the American pastor stood and gave a second invitation.

> "Jesus is the Answer. He answers prayers. Come, experience Him."

"For any of you who have prayer requests, please come forward so we can pray for your needs. Jesus is the Answer. He answers prayers. Come, experience Him."

My mind flicked back to my prayers to Allah. I prayed to him five times a day and still received no answer. Yet I remembered that I had prayed once to the God of Abraham, Isaac and Jacob—the God of Christians—and He had answered me. So when the pastor said, "Jesus is the Answer," that caught my attention and rang in my heart as true.

I'm a Muslim, but I can still receive prayer, I thought. *Why not?* I was searching for answers. Would the Christian God be able to make the war end? Could He bring peace?

I made my way to the front with many others. Turning to my right, I saw Gamila walking beside me. The congregation sang the songs "All Heaven Declares" and "Worthy Is the Lamb" as we walked down the aisle. My heart beat rapidly with fear as I wondered if any other Muslims might see me and recognize me in the crowd. But I also had a sense of expectation that something big was about to happen.

When I got to the front, the pastor placed his hand gently on my forehead to pray for me. As he did, a surge of warmth passed through me as the Holy Spirit touched me powerfully. I was unable to stand and fell to the ground. Not understanding what had happening, I tried to stand, but the weighty presence of God was too strong. I gave up and lay peacefully on the floor as warmth like soothing oil flowed through me.

As I lay there, I had a vision of Jesus—on the cross crucified. I began to weep as I saw His hands and feet pierced on the cross. My eyes were opened to the revelation of the enormity of what Jesus had done. As John 1:29 proclaims: "Behold, the Lamb of God who takes away the sin of the world!"

In the vision, God spoke to me and called me by name. "Mariam, you deserved to die for your sins, but I died instead of you so you will live. I set you free from your sin and shame. You are forgiven. Receive My love and forgiveness and stop striving for it. When you receive My love by faith, you will become My child."

The vision was so vivid that I could almost touch the blood dripping from His wounded head, hands, feet and side.

"Repent and turn to Me, and you will be with Me in Paradise because of what I have done by My grace. I took your shame so you are free from the judgment of hell and condemnation."

I started weeping afresh with this revelation of God's mercy. I felt as if I would explode with joy at the offering of this incredible gift (see James 1:17–18).

I understood that blood needed to be shed for our sins to be forgiven every year. Seventy days after Ramadan, we would make a sacrifice by killing a lamb. Every year, as the innocent lamb was taken to slaughter, I heard its terrified bleating and wept for the innocent animal. Now I knew my sins could not be cleansed by an animal sacrifice, but only by the ultimate sacrifice of Jesus.

As I lay there, I understood that God had given His precious Son to die for me. The cross turned from a symbol of death, where Jesus was crucified, to the symbol of love. It signified what Jesus had sacrificed for my sake—His very life. The Holy Spirit touched my heart as I realized that no one had died for me before. Not Muhammad, not Buddha, not Krishna. Only Jesus Christ had proven His love for me by shedding His precious blood for my sake. He died that I might live. Only true, pure love can sacrifice in such a way.

> No one had died for me before. Not Muhammad, not Buddha, not Krishna. Only Jesus Christ had proven His love for me by shedding His precious blood for my sake.

In the end, no person had to explain to me that Jesus was the Son of God. It was revealed to me by Jesus Himself.

He continued to speak to me. "My precious daughter, I chose you before the foundation of earth to be My princess. You are royalty even when you don't feel like a princess. I will wait for you until you are ready to start living the amazing plans I have for you. I know you don't know where to begin or how to become what I have called you to be, so let Me teach you every day. Start by recognizing who I am: King of kings and Lord of lords. The Lover of your soul. When the two of us meet alone together every day, I will show you how to let go of things in your life that are holding back blessings I want to give you."

His voice was soothing. "Remember, My child, just as I have chosen you, I have given you a choice to represent Me to the world. If you are willing, I will give you all you need to complete your calling. I am your King and Lord who chose you (see 1 Peter 2:9). You did not choose Me. I appointed you to go and produce fruit that will last so that the Father will give you whatever you ask for using My Name."

From that point on my life was His unconditionally. I had a deep understanding that He was my heavenly Father and I was the daughter of the King of kings. As John 1:12 says, "Yet to all who did receive him, to those who believed in his name, he gave the right to become children of God" (NIV).

I lay on the floor for hours, but it seemed as though only moments had passed.

When I was finally able to move, I rose a different person. I had been living in fear of man and death. Suddenly I had a new joy and boldness given to me in the baptism of the Holy Spirit (see Romans 8:14–16). I was delivered from nightmares.

I experienced the truth of 1 John 4:18—"Perfect love casts out fear," because fear left me for good when I asked Jesus into my heart. The root and stronghold of Islam is fear, but the Lord took away the spirit of fear and gave me a spirit of power.

For the first time I heard God speak. I was no longer having a monologue with Allah but a dialogue with my Creator! We had heart-to-heart communication, as a lamb does to the Shepherd (see John 10:27), and He was answering my prayers. Even though the war continued in my country, I instantly felt peace. That's because the Prince of Peace—Jesus—entered my heart and calmed all the storms.

> **I instantly felt peace because the Prince of Peace—Jesus—entered my heart and calmed all the storms.**

I looked around and saw Gamila. We walked toward one another. From the light in her eyes, I knew she also had been changed.

"What happened to you?" I asked her.

"I gave my life to Jesus." She laughed.

A minister took us to another room where he explained in our own language what had happened. He led us in the prayer of repentance. "Romans 10:9 says, 'If you declare with your mouth, "Jesus is Lord," and believe in your heart that God raised him from the dead, you will be saved'" (NIV).

Together Gamila and I prayed, "Heavenly Father, You know

I have sinned and am not worthy to be called Your child. But I believe You are a God of mercy and that You sent Your Son, Jesus, to die on the cross for my sins. So I turn to You, Lord Jesus, with great thankfulness. I surrender my life to You. I ask You to forgive me for all that is past, to cleanse me from all my sins and to give me Your Holy Spirit to live within me as my Teacher and my Friend. I reject Satan and every occult spirit and renounce the spirit of Islam in the name of Jesus Christ and declare the Word of God, 'If the Son has set you free, you are free indeed.' I declare that Jesus has set me free from all my sins, from every bondage of Satan. I have been born from on high. I am a child of God. I am a new creation. I have eternal life. In Jesus' mighty name, Amen. Hallelujah!"

Gamila and I were each given a New Testament and encouraged to read it every day. We were so excited as we walked home with Alim. He was overjoyed.

"There is a Bible study you can go to," he said, "and God will instruct you through His Word."

My heart was full. I couldn't wait to come back to church to worship the living God, the God of love.

> Love suffers long and is kind; love does not envy; love does not parade itself, is not puffed up; does not behave rudely, does not seek its own, is not provoked, thinks no evil; does not rejoice . in iniquity, but rejoices in the truth; bears all things, believes all things, hopes all things, endures all things. Love never fails. But whether there are prophecies, they will fail; whether there are tongues, they will cease; whether there is knowledge, it will vanish away.
>
> 1 Corinthians 13:4–8 NKJV

At the same time, I knew that what had just happened was going to change the course of my entire life . . . and my relationship with my family.

9

WALKING WITH JESUS

When I arrived home that day, I could not contain my excitement. I was radically changed, my face shone and I was smiling ear to ear. I felt I had come alive for the first time. At fourteen years old I was overwhelmed that Jesus loved me. I'd always felt that something was missing in my life, but try as I might, I could not find what it was. Now I knew only Jesus held the peace I'd been longing for.

Despite my transformation, my circumstances did not change. Our country was still at war. But instead of the fear I had constantly lived with, I now had a supernatural joy and the kind of peace the apostle John talks about:

> "Peace I leave with you; my peace I give you. I do not give to you as the world gives. Do not let your hearts be troubled and do not be afraid."
>
> John 14:27 NIV

My family had no idea what had happened, but I was in love with Jesus Christ. I couldn't hold the good news to myself. I wanted to tell the world about my dearly beloved Savior, starting with my family, relatives, friends and neighbors. But I also needed to be wise. I had to look for an opportunity—the right time and place. I couldn't tell them straightaway, because they would be horrified and forbid me from going back to church.

So I prayed for a way to share what I had found, relying on the Holy Spirit to lead me. He revealed to me that I needed to share with family, relatives, friends and all Muslims individually and be sensitive to the community culture. The pressure of community might get me killed, but one-on-one evangelism will save them.

As the days passed I devoured the New Testament I'd been given. I hid it under my coat and then locked myself in the bathroom so I could pore over the pages without fear of being caught. My family sometimes banged on the door and shouted at me to get out if I had been in there for too long. Quickly making some excuse, I would tuck the Bible back under my clothing and open the door, waiting for the next opportunity I could take to read it. I didn't have a place to pray at the house, so I prayed in the shower. I just let the water run as I prayed and sang in the Spirit.

I started going to church every Sunday, walking with Gamila and Alim, and was welcomed again with such love by the congregation. Every week I eagerly took in all I was taught in the sermons.

One of the interior walls of the building had Jeremiah 33:3 painted on it: "Call to Me, and I will answer you, and show you great and mighty things, which you do not know" (NKJV). The verse became like a heavenly command as I called on the name of the Lord and asked Him to reveal His truth to me.

I learned from James 5:16 about the power of prayer: "The prayer of a righteous person is powerful and effective" (NIV). I knew I was now righteous in God's sight because my sins had been forgiven by Jesus' death on the cross, so I kept on pouring out my heart to my Savior, asking for my family's salvation. I understood I had to prepare a way for them to be able to receive Jesus.

Even though at first I didn't tell my family what had happened, my actions spoke louder than words. I changed dramatically. As the weeks went by, I no longer prayed to Allah five times a day or went to the Mullah as I had. I was now in a love relationship with my Creator, and I prayed to Him in my own language. The Mullah obviously noticed my absence and sent my fellow pupils to ask why I wasn't coming to the lessons. I just told them I didn't want to go to lessons anymore.

> **I no longer prayed to Allah five times a day. I was now in a love relationship with my Creator.**

I was no longer striving for acceptance and approval from the people around me. My fear of what others thought of me had left, because I was now living to an audience of One—I just wanted to please my Beloved.

As a sign of my new freedom I even stopped wearing the Islamic outfit for women and the veil over my head. Being the youngest child, I usually had favor in my family to do whatever I wanted, but there was still a battle for them to understand or agree to me not covering my hair in public.

As I stood my ground, I remembered 1 Samuel 16:7: "The LORD does not look at the things people look at. People look at the outward appearance, but the LORD looks at the heart" (NIV).

I told my parents: "I want to please God more than people; I want to fear Him more than man. And He looks at my heart, not at my religious activities."

The Lord told me to *be* the message to my family—to practically show them the love of Jesus. Following His example of being the Servant of all, I started to serve them—cleaning the house, running errands for my mother and loving my brothers and sisters with all of my being. As Mark 10:45 says: "For even the Son of Man did not come to be served, but to serve, and to give His life a ransom for many." Before I became a Christian, my family members served me. But when I began to serve them, they were amazed. Their hearts started to melt from experiencing the kind of love that serves sacrificially.

> **The Lord told me to be the message to my family—to practically show them the love of Jesus.**

A New Identity

I knew the ministry of Jesus was the ministry of servanthood, and I wanted to be like Him. Before my conversion, I had been hanging out with friends on our street who swore a lot, and I had fallen into the habit of using bad language. Overnight this stopped.

When I had the revelation of Jesus, He spoke to me about having a new identity in Him, and that He was going to give me a new name. I was being made new, and I understood the words from 2 Corinthians 5:17—"Therefore if anyone is in Christ, the new creation has come: The old has gone, the new is here!" (NIV).

Names are very significant in Middle-Eastern culture. I believe they represent nature and are prophetic. What you are called, you are destined to become. In Genesis 17:5 God changed Abram's name (meaning "Exalted Father") to Abraham, meaning "Father of many"—this was his inheritance. The Lord also changed his wife's name from Sarai to Sarah (verse 15). Sarai means

"Argumentative," but then God changed the last two letters to *ah*, a symbol of His breath. The *ah* of Jehovah makes Sarai new. Her identity is changed: Sarah means "Princess." She is the daughter of the King. Jesus also renewed the names of His disciples, especially the three closest to Him, including Simon to Peter the Rock.

It's amazing to me that God speaks even in the names of the genealogy:

Adam means "Man"

Seth means "Appointed"

Enosh means "Mortal"

Cainan means "Sorrow"

Mahalalel means "Blessed God"

Jared means "Shall come down"

Enoch means "Teaching"

Methuselah means "His death shall bring"

Lamech means "The Despairing"

Noah means "Comfort-Rest"

Names are very significant in Middle-Eastern culture. I believe they represent nature and are prophetic. What you are called, you are destined to become.

A Man, Appointed and Mortal, bearing Sorrow, Blessed God, Shall come down, Teaching, and His death shall Bring the Despairing Comfort and Rest = Jesus! YHWH-YAHWEH, meaning "Behold the hand, behold the nail!"

On the day I invited Jesus into my heart, He told me I had a new identity in Him. I wondered what my new name was, but I didn't have long to find out. God revealed it to me first and then confirmed it through my friend Munira. She prophesied that I had a new name, and that it was Samaa.

Samaa, meaning "Heaven, Paradise"—a place everyone wants to go.

I knew straightaway that the name was from God because He had already been speaking to me about it. Whenever I read the word *heaven* in the Bible it jumped out at me. So when Munira said the name, my heart started beating faster, and I had a sense of peace that this was His name for me. I already had the assurance of heaven through believing in Jesus Christ. The name *Samaa* spoke of my calling to tell people about the heavenly paradise waiting for those who believe.

When Munira and other friends began to introduce me to everyone in church as Samaa, the name stuck.

However, when I told my family that God had given me a new name, and that I wanted them to call me Samaa, they couldn't understand.

"What?" exclaimed my father. "I named you *Mariam,* and that is what you are called, *not* Samaa!"

My mother was exasperated, too, telling me my father had chosen such a beautiful name and that I was ungrateful to reject it. "Just wait 'til you have children and they do this to you. *Then* you will understand!"

"Mama, I have to obey God," was all I could reply.

My whole family fought my new choice of name—they got very frustrated with me when I would only answer to Samaa and not the name I was given at birth. However, as time went by and they saw how serious I was, they slowly gave in and began to call me by my new heavenly name.

"It's a Miracle!"

I was still secretly reading the New Testament that the church had given me every moment I could. I would hide it under my pillow and read it morning and night. I read in Romans 14:11:

"Every knee shall bow to Me, and every tongue shall confess to God" (NKJV). I was now acknowledging that Jesus is my Lord in my mother tongue.

As I tried to walk out my new faith with my family, God healed my body. I had always been sickly, often getting colds and headaches and goiters. I prayed for Jesus to heal me as I suffered from tiredness and pain throughout my body and found it hard to catch my breath. My mother had even recently taken me to the hospital, fearing I had inherited the heart problem that had killed her father.

After inviting Jesus into my life, all of my symptoms left. I felt strong physically and could breathe normally.

"I am healed!" I told my mother.

Before she would even think about letting me throw away my medication, Mama insisted I go back to the doctor to be tested.

When we were able to get to the hospital, the doctor pronounced me 100 percent fit and had no explanation for my sudden recovery.

"It's a miracle!" she said as she led us out of her office.

I was not surprised by my healing. I assumed it was normal. Had not Jesus said in Mark 16:18, "They will place their hands on sick people and they will get well"? (NIV). Since becoming a Christian, I had already seen many miracles. I even went to the hospitals in our city with Rasul, meaning "Messenger," an evangelist from church. We saw many healed, and because of it were asked to come back by the Muslim doctors. People with chronic illnesses, blindness, lameness, infertility and heart problems were all healed in Jesus' name. I had a simple faith and was just doing what Jesus told me to do. As He promised in Mark 16:17, "Signs will accompany those who believe" (NIV).

10

SUPERNATURAL STRENGTH

Gamila and I were practicing our throwing and falling techniques. This was my least favorite set of exercises, but one of the most important to execute properly, because of the lack of mats in the gym. If we landed incorrectly, we could be injured.

I was not afraid of being hurt, but I was afraid that if I broke my wrist or sprained my knee my parents would make me stop coming to class!

After a hip throw, in which I planted Gamila on the floor while keeping control of her hand, she bounded up at once and said, "My turn!"

I must not have been paying proper attention because, instead of bouncing like a rubber ball, I hit flat on my back with a thud, with the air knocked out of me. Coach came over to me and helped me sit up and then stand.

In his typical, low-key way, he offered me correction. While I watched, he went through the proper technique in slow motion, then repeated it, allowing Gamila to flip him onto the floor.

He stood, smiling with genuine reassurance. The more I got to know this man, the more I liked him—not only as a strong person but because of how much he loved his friend Jesus. He had also shared with me that our pastor had been beaten for his faith. Further, he and the coach had been threatened many times: "If you won't get out of our country, you'll be killed."

> The more I got to know this man, the more I liked him— not only as a strong person but because of how much he loved his friend Jesus.

However, he told me, "My Christian faith teaches me not to be afraid of them who can kill the body. The Bible says: 'Greater is he who is in you'—that means Jesus—'than he who is in the world' (1 John 4:4). I'm not afraid, and neither should you be."

Neither my pastor nor coach had to be here. It was not their home country. Yet they stayed because of their faith in Jesus Christ.

The First Competition

In order to progress from one rank to the next in tae kwon do, we had to pass a series of exams. These opportunities only came around twice each year and were always connected with competition.

I was very nervous as the time for my first competition approached. I knew my parents would not be present, since both of them hated fighting, but several of my brothers and sisters planned to attend. I wanted to do well and uphold the family honor.

What I had not realized is how many of the people of our town had heard about the event and wanted to see for themselves what this tae kwon do sport was like.

When the rest of the competitors and I emerged from the locker room, the gym overflowed with hundreds of spectators—filling all the seats, standing along every wall and peering into the interior around each doorjamb!

I suddenly had a huge flock of butterflies in my stomach. I had no idea that so many people would turn out to see the competition. But as soon as we completed our warm-ups, including a time of prayer, and the matches began, my nervousness left. It did not matter that hundreds of people were watching. I had studied. I had trained. I had a goal to pass the exams and earn my belt . . . and I did.

The Second Competition

Even after the civil war ended, my country was still a very lawless place. Walking in the dark to early morning prayer meetings and Friday night gatherings added to the danger for me. The nighttime streets were still empty of people and cars. No one left their homes after sunset because of the risk of being attacked.

But I was in love with Jesus, and sometimes that love made me do things I wouldn't otherwise have done. It made me brave.

I was sixteen years old and had been studying tae kwon do for a couple of years. I had passed the tests to achieve first my yellow and then my green belts.

Johnny's schools had multiplied all over our country. Even though all the classes operated as mini-churches, hundreds of Muslims came to learn self-defense. Many stayed to meet and receive Jesus as Savior and Lord, despite the fact they would be persecuted by their families and suffer beatings. Others would receive death threats.

The time came for another set of tae kwon do exams and another competition. I had faced this challenge before, but I was nervous about demonstrating my mastery of technical terms, as well as kicks and punches, and then the matches.

Hundreds of students were at this gathering. We had worship, a sermon, then the exams, followed by the prize ceremony. More and more participants had acquired proper tae kwon do gear. We made an impressive show for hundreds and hundreds of onlookers as we stood in the gym in our black-and-white uniforms, set off with a rainbow of colored belts of rank.

At the conclusion of the exams and matches, I had passed to the next level of training and was awarded my blue belt. I was thrilled.

I was an eager and enthusiastic student, applying myself with great diligence. Very few of us beginners had or could afford the traditional yellow or green belts, but from the very start I saw the advanced students who came to demonstrate various techniques. I set a goal of earning one of the black belts as soon as possible.

Because the whole event involved so many athletes, the day's activities did not end until nearly dark. Nor were the concluding ceremonies the end of my day. I needed to rush home and change and then go out to church. Our Friday night praise and worship time that began at 10:00 p.m. would continue until 5:00 a.m.!

A Shocking Encounter

Some friends and I were fortunate to catch the only public transport available: a minibus jammed with folks who did not want to travel by foot at night. Several of us journeyed together until one friend and I had to change to a different minibus, so we were separated from the others.

At a later stop I parted from my friend at a location about twenty minutes' walk from my home, while she motored on closer to her destination. "Are you sure you'll be okay?" she asked.

I assured her I'd be fine. We hugged good-bye, congratulating each other on our success, and then I hurried off into the night.

Wearing jeans and a white sweatshirt, I clutched my gym bag containing my tae kwon do uniform and my New Testament. I didn't need a coat, because the air was quite warm.

Almost immediately after the minibus drove off and disappeared around a corner it began to rain. Fat drops landed on my face and eyelids. As I brushed them away, I noticed a tall, well-built man approaching me. He appeared to be in his mid-twenties.

> **Quietly I asked the Lord for protection and for His guidance in how to handle this situation.**

Two sensations swept over me. I knew he was dangerous and his intentions were not good, yet at the same time I had peace, which I recognized as a gift from God.

"Hey," he said, pausing beside me as I passed him. "Do you want me to walk with you? I can make sure you get safely to where you're going."

"It's okay," I returned. "Thank you, but I'll walk by myself."

I hoped he'd go away and leave me alone, but he insisted on tagging along after me. "No, I'll come with you."

"I'd rather you didn't," I said. "Please don't follow me."

He did not listen. When I quickened my pace, so did he.

"Hey, wait up," he demanded.

The rain fell harder now, splashing against the sidewalk and spattering my jeans. The pavement glistened, but the night grew darker and darker. Quietly I asked the Lord for protection and for His guidance in how to handle this situation.

Suddenly it came to me that I should speak to the man about God. "Do you know where you're going to go when you die?" I asked him.

"Heaven, I hope," he retorted.

"Great! Then you know the way to heaven?" Without waiting for another response, I told him that Jesus died for his sins. I explained that Jesus was the ultimate sacrifice and the only way to heaven. I continued my witnessing while continuing to walk briskly. We neared my home but had to go through an area between two buildings that was pitch black. As we entered the darkest stretch, he grabbed me, making me drop my gym bag and Bible. Pushing me up against a tree, he tried to rip my clothes off. I struggled with him, but he was bigger and stronger.

Part of me was shocked that he assaulted me while I spoke of Holy God! Hadn't he heard anything I'd said? But as Ezekiel 12:2 says, "You are living among a rebellious people. They have eyes to see but do not see and ears to hear but do not hear, for they are a rebellious people" (NIV).

From the earliest moments of my Christian life I had experienced Jesus answering my prayers. I wholeheartedly believed Psalm 46:1: "God is our refuge and strength, an ever-present help in trouble" (NIV).

I cried out to the Lord inwardly. *Help me!*

At that moment my attacker's hand clamped over my mouth. But God filled me with supernatural strength like that possessed by David when he fought the giant Goliath:

> David said to the Philistine, "You come against me with sword and spear and javelin, but I come against you in the name of the LORD Almighty, the God of the armies of Israel, whom you have defied."
>
> 1 Samuel 17:45 NIV

Just as David was able to defeat his giant with only his hands and five stones, I fought back with a might that was not mine. I not only fought for my purity but for my life! I drove the heel of my hand up into his chin. Seizing his wrist, I wrenched his grip off me, then spun him around. I saw a startled look in his eyes. Stumbling, his feet slipped on the wet pavement as I shoved him away.

In no time at all I freed myself from the man and then ran as fast as I could. I didn't stop until I reached home. My tae kwon do outfit and New Testament were lost, but I was safe.

I steadied myself before entering my home. I shook from the shock of the encounter but was afraid to tell my parents about my experience, fearing they would not let me go out at night anymore. I wanted to be able to come and go so I could get to our Friday night prayer session in a few hours. Every Friday the Muslims went to the mosque to pray, and that is why our church put on the weekly Friday nights of prayer—to intercede for our brothers and sisters who did not know Jesus. I was still planning to go with my sisters. We would wait until everyone in the apartment was asleep before sneaking out and heading there.

That very night my sisters and I used the same route on which I had been attacked. I hoped to find my bag with the expensive uniform, a gift from my brother Musa, and my precious New Testament. Despite reentering the darkness under the tree, I didn't find anything except a string torn from the hood of my sweatshirt. I prayed my assailant would read my Bible, if he had taken it, and get saved.

During the testimony time, I stood and told the congregation how the Lord had protected me and strengthened me and delivered me. I quoted Psalm 121:1: "I lift up my eyes to the mountains—where does my help come from? My help comes from the LORD, the Maker of heaven and earth" (NIV). Truly He was with me that night!

The Confrontation

A few months after the Lord gave me the Holy Spirit power to defend against my attacker in the dark street, I had another similar occasion to call on Him for help. Iman and I, together with another friend, went out to purchase fabric for my sister Malika to make me a tae kwon do uniform.

As we walked the streets, three big guys started whistling and calling to us: "Hey, beautiful girls." They were laughing.

At first we ignored them, but they followed us, making comments that grew ever more aggressive in tone.

God told me not to run. Instead I heard a voice instruct me to face them.

"Hey, stop! Come with us. We'll show you a good time. Even if you have boyfriends, that doesn't mean anything. Don't you want real men like us?"

God told me not to run. Instead I heard a voice instruct me to face them.

"Stop it!" I ordered. "Go away!"

One of them shook his hand derisively and grinned even wider. "What do you mean? You're three girls. We're three boys. It's perfect. Come on. What do you say?"

In Muslim countries women without male chaperones are the targets of assault. Since we had no men to protect us, these thugs felt they could easily do what they wanted with us.

Passersby who witnessed what was happening crossed the street to avoid being caught in the confrontation. There would be no help from any of them.

I saw fear in Iman's eyes.

One of the other males spoke directly to her. "You, sweet thing. Don't be so shy. If you show me a good time, I'll do the same for you. Come on. Don't pretend you don't want it."

Iman cowered behind me.

There was no police to call, no one to whom we could turn for help, except the Lord. I understood that we were engaged in a spiritual battle as well as a physical one. I began to pray in heavenly language in the Spirit.

Avoiding eye contact, trying to walk forward, Iman flinched when the same boy pinched her, then grabbed her. She flailed at him, but I saw his face harden with lust.

Under my breath I rebuked the demonic influence that had its hold on him. The other two men ringed us in, herding us together. They were trying to back us into an alley.

Suddenly the same fire I experienced that night after the tae kwon do competition came over me again. Once more I felt supernatural strength. As the men closed in and started to attack us, I attacked them back.

My legs swirled in perfectly executed kicks. My hands started fighting back all of them. My feet and hands were flying in all directions.

> There was no police to call, no one to whom we could turn for help, except the Lord. I understood that we were engaged in a spiritual battle as well as a physical one.

A crowd of onlookers, who would not have lifted a finger to save us, gathered around to watch.

"Look at her!" one bystander shouted. "She's a ninja!"

"She's Superwoman," another exclaimed.

Swinging into a high kick, I followed up with a combination of karate chops and punches. My foot made contact with an attacker's nose, and his hands grabbed his face as blood spurted.

Another got my fist in his ear, making him howl with pain.

My audience was cheering and applauding. "Keep going, Superwoman! Take them apart!"

"Amazing! Never saw anything like it!"

The third of the attackers, the one who pinched Iman, tried to duck away from a strike by the side of my fist. As he stooped,

I whirled. My heel caught him right on the point of the chin and sent him sprawling.

Just that quickly, it was over.

The three men, thoroughly defeated and embarrassed, backed away in shame. One held his bleeding nose. One clasped his ear and squinted with pain. Together they tried to support the third of the trio, who looked dazed and barely able to walk.

As the crowd jeered and laughed, the leader of the attackers vowed meekly, "We will never touch girls again. Honest, we won't."

Then the three men edged away from the smirking crowd.

As my pulse rate returned to normal, I discovered I was as amazed as everyone else. Taking a deep breath, I thanked God for His help and miraculous assistance.

Those who had seen the encounter continued to call out their approval and good wishes. "Well done, Superwoman!"

"You should be a coach. You should be training all the young women and girls. Make the streets safe!"

Eventually I would earn my black belt, become a coach and share the Gospel the same way that I was saved.

A Faith That Never Gives Up

Another time on a Friday my friend Munira and I were trying to get to church. At this time in our city there was intermittent public transport. Buses and taxis occasionally ran. We decided to wait at the bus stop in the hope that one might come. We waited, and we waited, but no bus came. Eventually we saw a car being driven toward us.

The vehicle slowed down and pulled over.

I had an uneasy feeling.

Sensing danger, Munira and I started walking away, when suddenly men with guns got out of the car. Since they obviously weren't police but they were carrying guns, we assumed they were criminals. They shouted at us to come with them. I knew what they were going to do; we had heard enough stories of the brutal rapes and murders. Clutching each other's hands, Munira and I tried to make a run for it, but it was too late. We were both grabbed by the men and dragged toward the waiting car, its engine still running.

Again I cried out to God, and as I did, the Holy Spirit fell on me. I was praying in heavenly language as I hit and punched, using karate kicks and tae kwon do moves. In a few minutes I got free and thought Munira was, too. I started running, but as I looked back, I saw my friend, paralyzed by fear and unable to fight or run, being bundled into the car.

> I realized that even though the men had guns, they hadn't shot at us. I knew that this was God. He had again protected us.

"Munira," I shouted, running back. I couldn't leave her.

With a supernatural strength that was not mine, I grabbed Munira and tried to pull her from their clutches. It was a real fight, but eventually we were both free, although bruised and bleeding. We ran as fast as we could out of the area. Later I realized that even though the men had guns, they hadn't shot at us. I knew that this was God. He had again protected us.

The Lord says in Zechariah 4:6, "Not by might nor by power, but by my Spirit" (NIV). I had experienced that same power, and it had saved my friend and me from the clutches of evil men.

Despite the very real danger on the streets, I never stopped going to church or tae kwon do.

Faith never gives up! I would tell myself. My hunger for truth and fellowship was bigger than my fear.

Mercy over Judgment

Restoration after the war took a long time, but slowly things became normal again. One day, after the police began maintaining better order again, I was in a market with my sister Adila, and my expensive cell phone was stolen. I ran fast enough to catch the thief, but he had thrown my phone to another member of his gang who was able to get away. I took the main thief to the police to bring justice upon injustice. The police interrogated him, but he did not identify the rest of the gang or give up where the phone might be. The police kept him in jail for a few nights.

A couple days later my doorbell rang, and I opened it to find the mother of the thief. She had gotten my address from the police. She began to weep bitterly, begging me to have mercy on her son and tell the police to release him from jail. Just as I had experienced how God's mercy triumphs over judgment, I extended mercy to her and her son—with the condition that they come to church with me for a month. They agreed, and I was able to share the Gospel with them, praying that God's love would turn hearts of stone to hearts of flesh.

11

THE COST OF FOLLOWING JESUS

All during the war we knew that if the Muslim Brotherhood won, our country would become a strict Islamic nation ruled by Sharia Law. This would affect women the most as we would not be able to get jobs, drive or even walk alone in the street. And we'd always have to wear the burka covering our whole body.

There was nothing we could do to stop the fighting except pray, so our church, along with many others, fasted for the country's freedom and for the civil war to end. My pastor felt we needed to pray and fast for our nation for 21 days, so different members of the congregation would take spans of days during this time—some one to three days, some seven, some ten, some the whole 21 days . . . however they felt led by the Lord.

When the three-week period was up, we sensed the prayer should not stop, so we continued to pray and fast for 24 hours a day, seven days a week. I would pray for four to seven hours each day, crying out to God to have mercy on our nation.

This rhythm of prayer and fasting ended up going on for

several years, with members taking shifts all through the day and night.

God heard our cries. After five years of war, our country was given religious freedom. Out of a population of approximately six million, an estimated 150,000 people, mostly civilians, had been killed. Some 1.5 million had been displaced internally, driven from their homes, and had escaped into neighboring countries as refugees.

Officially, the civil war had ended, but there were still armed clashes between renegade forces. The country

God heard our cries.

was now limping after years of fighting. Life would not seem "normal" for a long time. The consequences of war meant there was still little food, only intermittent power in our homes, curfews, and always danger on the streets.

As there had been no school during the war we had a home-school system set up. Teachers who lived nearby would try to help us, and my mother also taught us.

When the war was over, schools opened again, and I was able to get my high school diploma. My passion was to learn languages, and I applied for a place at the university to study languages and computers. I couldn't wait to be able to talk to people from different cultures.

However, there was a problem—I could not afford to study, as my parents had no money left. So I asked God to provide and held on to the promise in Philippians 4:19: "And my God will meet all your needs according to the riches of his glory in Christ Jesus."

Our church had a visiting Bible teacher from Asia at that time. He was a very kind man, and although he had seven sons, he had no daughters. This man treated me like his daughter and cared for me in such a way that I felt it was God showing His Father's heart for me.

Retreat in the Mountains

The following October I went with Adila and Malika for a second year to the retreat camp in the mountains. This time we were there to serve. Iman went as a candidate, as she had been baptized in the summer.

While we were there, the Bible teacher asked me about my plans for the future, and I told him about my dreams for further education. He listened to me intently, and then to my surprise said he wanted to make a way for me to continue my studies. He offered to pay all my tuition fees.

> **It was such a generous gift, revealing God's faithfulness to me once more.**

I was amazed, and tears came to my eyes. It was such a generous gift, revealing God's faithfulness to me once more. My sisters and I came home from the retreat on a spiritual high.

Then, immediately, the enemy tried to steal our joy through our brother Musa. He had been suspicious of our camping trip and through other people in the community had learned what it entailed.

The following Sunday he went to church to find us.

The service that day was a real celebration as we gave testimonies of what God had done in our lives at the retreat. Adila and I were in the choir, so an usher came to tell Malika that our brother was in the building looking for us.

Malika dared not turn around. She knew what was coming.

Musa would not come into the sanctuary, not wanting to defile himself, but stayed in the corridor. At the end of the service Adila, Malika, Iman and I went out to meet him. When I saw the anger in his face, I knew we were in for another beating.

116

"Why are you not obeying me? I told you *not* to go," he hissed, spitting with rage.

As I prayed under my breath, we descended the three flights of stairs out into the fresh air.

Then Musa let loose. He started dragging us along the road by our clothes and hair. "What did you do at this camp? And why are you still going to church and recruiting more of your siblings?" he demanded as he hit us.

I cried, begging him to let us go. Without mercy he grabbed me and then punched me hard in the face. I fell to the ground at the impact. The pain was mind-numbing, and I felt sticky blood flow from my nose.

Other members who had followed us outside tried to intervene. "Aren't you afraid of God?" they said to him, trying to pull him off us.

"It's none of your business! I'll beat you, too, if you don't shut your mouths and stop trying to help them," Musa furiously shouted.

We took public transport home, all of us girls sitting in silence, with Musa issuing threats. When we eventually got to our apartment, he violently took my head and smashed it against the wall. I nearly passed out, but Musa just moved on to the next sister to do the same thing.

"You stubborn girls," he screamed. "Why aren't you listening to me?"

Musa felt humiliated by us. He was desperate to bring us all back together as Muslims and would do whatever he needed in order for this to happen. "Why are you bringing shame on the family?" he asked over and over again.

We were black and blue by the time he had finished with us, but our resolve was not shaken. We were willing to put up with beatings for the sake of Jesus. Jesus was worth it all.

Over the next few weeks Musa's anger was still simmering,

> **We braced ourselves to face more beatings if this was the cost of following Jesus.**

and we all tried to keep out of his way. Mama begged us to do what he said, but I explained to her that we could not. We braced ourselves to face more beatings if this was the cost of following Jesus. We clung to 2 Corinthians 1:5: "For just as we share abundantly in the sufferings of Christ, so also our comfort abounds through Christ" (NIV).

An Unshakable Faith

At about that time the UN and Red Cross came into the country to help our nation recuperate after the war. Volunteers from both agencies took English classes at my university, as many professionals and teachers had either been killed or had left the country. I was thrilled to be able to practice speaking to foreigners.

My university was my mission field since most of my classmates were Muslim.

I wrote a list of everyone in my class, then shared the Gospel with them, and fasted and prayed for them. Some of my classmates became Christians. One of my teachers at the college was an English man. I told him about the love of Jesus and he came to church with me on Sunday. He even participated in the Friday night prayer, staying until we finished at 5:00 a.m.

A beautiful girl named Uzma, meaning "Supreme, greatest," seemed untouched by my prayers. She appeared arrogant and ignored me whenever I tried to tell her about Jesus. I kept praying, hoping that one day her heart would soften.

A couple of years later I walked into church one Sunday morning and there, in front of me, was Uzma. "What are you doing here?" I exclaimed in surprise.

She told me she had met a Christian man and fallen in love. Through him she had become a believer, and they had recently married. Tears came to her eyes as I told her I had been praying for her every day. I was crying, too, and we hugged each other, amazed at what God had done. She was not the only one of my classmates who came to know the Lord.

After I had been at my university for a year, the foreign lecturers were suddenly kicked out over our spring holiday. We returned to classes to find only the local teachers were left. We were never told the reason the lecturers went, but I could no longer study there because all my language teachers had gone. But when God shuts a window, He opens a door!

My dream now was to go to the College for International Relations. The College for International Relations was the top university in our country, and I thought it was completely out of my reach. I still had the financial backing of the Bible teacher, but I had yet to pass the entry exam. I made an appointment to see the president of the university and boldly told him I wanted to study international relations. I asked if it would be possible to take the exam. I had ambitions to work as a diplomat, a peacemaker.

When God shuts a window, He opens a door!

The president allowed me to take the test. I passed and was given a place at the university. It was a miracle! Never in my wildest dreams had I imagined I would have a place provided for me at such a prestigious institution. Again it was a sign of God's faithfulness. I recognized Him as *Jehovah-Jirah*, which is Hebrew for "God my Provider."

My life was busy and full. Yet, in contrast to the freedom and hope provided by my studies, my sisters and I were still being persecuted by my family. The worst beatings were from Musa, whose temper was terrifying. He and Suleyman both had their own houses now because they were married, but sometimes they would turn up at our home on Sundays, as they knew that was the day we would try to go to church. If we were not at home when they arrived, they waited until we returned and would demand to know where we had been. Whatever we said made them angry, but we never retaliated or fought back.

By now my sisters and I were completely rejected by our Muslim neighbors, friends and relatives. They all knew we had converted from Islam to Christianity because we had not been afraid to share our new faith with them.

In our city it was common for people to congregate outside in the streets in the late afternoon to chat, eat pistachio nuts and drink tea. During those times my sisters and I used to take any opportunity to talk about Jesus.

Even though many were touched and intrigued by our words, the majority rebuked us, calling us the infidel. They would pick up stones and threaten to hit us as we walked by. They never hurt us, but instead put pressure on the male members of our family to take a stand against us. My brothers were mocked constantly, their friends asking, "Are you not the men of your house?"

However, despite the persecution we were under, people in our community did become Christians. One neighbor suffered a mental illness. He had nightmares every night, and no one could cure him. We invited him to church, and Adila shared the Gospel with him. When she prayed for his healing, he was completely restored and delivered.

We never gave up sharing about Jesus. Though persecution is the price we paid, we still had joy and a peace that was unshakable.

12

Supernatural Bodyguard

When a Muslim becomes a Christian, he or she is radical in their faith. The cost to serve Jesus is high, but there is so much joy and freedom in choosing Him that even if it costs you your life, the reward far outweighs the sacrifice.

My sisters and I would wake at 4:00 a.m. to run to the prayer meeting, praying in heavenly language the whole way for our safety. Nothing would stop us—not rain, snow or war. We went because we loved to be free in the presence of God while at home we had to hide our faith.

Our mother knew where we were going, but our father and brothers had no idea. They woke up early to go to work and assumed we were still asleep in our beds.

When we arrived at church, our coach would take the tae kwon do students through fitness training from 6:00–7:00 a.m. During that time we ran around our city in our white tae kwon do uniforms, shouting out Bible verses. I would yell at the top of my voice, "I can do all things through Christ who strengthens me!" (Philippians 4:13 NKJV). At this time the war was not so intense in our city, so being on the streets in the early morning was not too dangerous.

Most forms of martial arts have long histories of eastern religious influence. However, the tae kwon do philosophy was established in the 1950s by the South Korean army for self-defense and combat techniques. Tae kwon do includes "love and benevolence, magnanimity, sympathy and character as well as the five tenets of tae kwon do: courtesy, integrity, perseverance, self-control and an indomitable spirit."

The American missionary who came to my country felt that tae kwon do could be used as a suitable, effective way to model discipleship and promote Christianity. The Lord gives talents and gifts, and even sport can be used to advance His Kingdom. As it says in Acts 1:8 (NIV):

> "But you will receive power when the Holy Spirit comes on you; and you will be my witnesses in Jerusalem, and in all Judea and Samaria, and to the ends of the earth."

To respond to this prophetic command our church put on crusades in the streets. We visited hospitals, boldly preaching about the God of the Bible. With all the prayer and worship at church we had been infused with the Holy Spirit to go to our city and villages and tell people about Jesus. We were sent out two by two for local outreach and would go on mission trips, as described in Luke 10:1, 4:

We were like the disciples, taking no food or money with us.

> The Lord appointed seventy others, and sent them in pairs ahead of Him to every city and place where He Himself was going to come. . . . "Carry no money belt, no bag, no shoes; and greet no one on the way."

When we traveled, we were like the disciples, taking no food or money with us (see Mark 6:8). In each province we visited we would ask the Lord which house to go to. We would then knock on the door and talk to the people. Because of the culture of hospitality to strangers, we were invited in and given food to eat and a place to sleep for the night. The people were so hospitable that they gave us their beds and slept on the floor.

> **Despite the persecution, we saw much fruit and many people came to the Lord on our different trips.**

However, when we told the residents why we were there, we often faced persecution and the abusive shouts of angry Mullahs. Many times we were chased out of villages and almost stoned. Once when I was with a group of about seven others we ate a meal with the villagers and then began to share why we had come.

On hearing we were Christians they got very angry and shouted at us to leave immediately. We had no option but to go, and quickly, as they were already picking up stones to throw at us. It was sad when this happened, but we were guided by the words in Matthew 10:14: "If anyone will not welcome you or listen to your words, leave that home or town and shake the dust off your feet" (NIV). So we just prayed for them and moved on.

Another time a whole village came out in a riot against us with sticks and other weapons. We had to run for our lives, but before we could escape, we were arrested by a policeman who accused us of stirring up tension. He wanted a bribe for our release, but instead we gave him pamphlets containing the Gospel message and used the opportunity to share our testimonies. In the end he set us free. His heart was touched by the truth and love of the Lord, even inviting us back to eat with his family before we left.

Despite the persecution, we saw much fruit and many people came to the Lord on our different trips.

Surprising Deliverances

Adila loved these mission trips, as she was passionate about preaching. She took a mission trip with Nuh to a different region, where there was a mini-revival. Four hundred people not only heard the Gospel but were healed and delivered, including a girl who was demon-possessed. When the mission team spoke through a translator in the language of the people, the demon-possessed girl responded with a male voice, and in our language—one that she did not know—saying, "Jesus is in you." They cast the demon out of her, delivering her and setting her free. She came to church and eventually married a Christian man.

One day, when Adila and Malika were going to church, they were chased by gangster boys. Adila prayed, and the Lord gave her an idea to pretend that she had a gun in her purse. She said to Malika, "I'm going to pull out my gun and shoot all of these guys who want to harm us." The gangster boys started running away. Again, God supernaturally protected them.

Again, God supernaturally protected them.

When our church planted a new congregation in the outskirts of our city, Adila went with a team for a five-day mission, doing street evangelism and preaching. The team saw many healings, and people gave their lives to the Lord.

At the end of the week Adila wanted to get back to the Friday prayer night. She traveled in a bus part of the way with another girl, but her friend wanted to go to her home to shower before going to the meeting. She told Adila at which stop to get off and gave my sister directions to get to church. Then she left.

It was dark by the time Adila got off the bus, and although she had tried to take in the directions, she soon got lost. Suddenly a man in military uniform carrying a gun came up to her.

"Hey, who are you?" he said, trying to grab her hand. "Come talk to me."

Adila shook him off and kept walking, but she was still lost.

The man did not give up trying to touch her. He rubbed up against her and attempted to kiss her.

"Get off me," she shouted. "It's a sin to do that!"

Adila hated injustice, and a righteous anger rose in her at how the man treated her. She shared the Gospel with him, telling him to repent. Her words were so strong that he gave up and walked away, but not before she gave him a tract with the Gospel message to take with him.

As my sister continued on the lonely road, lost and alone, she felt fear. Knowing that fear comes to steal God's blessings, Adila started praying for the Lord's help.

Another man walked toward her. When he came closer, he asked where she was going and why she was out at night. It was dangerous, he said.

He was tall and strong. He spoke well and looked educated and respectable. She felt she could trust him.

"I'm lost. I'm trying to get to church. Can you give me directions?" she asked, telling him the street on which the building was located.

"I know that place," the man agreed. "I'll walk you there, but will you do me a favor first?" He said he was leaving the city and wanted to go to his girlfriend's flat. He asked Adila to come with him to her home, and then he, with his girlfriend, would take Adila to church. He said her house was on the way.

Because Adila felt comfortable with him, she agreed, and on the journey shared her faith in Jesus. He seemed interested and asked my sister many questions, keeping her talking. She was so happy sharing her faith that she took no notice of how far they had gone.

Suddenly Adila realized the man had brought her to a bad area of town. She started to feel uneasy. "When will we get to your girlfriend's house?" she asked.

"We're almost there. Almost there," he replied, walking on.

Eventually they came to a hole in a wall that led into a wasteland area, without houses or people.

"This is the way—go through," he said.

Adila felt the Holy Spirit warning her, but she didn't know what to do. As they walked through into an empty field her heart sank. The man had tricked her. She knew then he planned to rape her. Sure enough, he calmly said: "So, can I sleep with a Christian?"

Adila felt the Holy Spirit warning her.

"No!" replied Adila in horror.

"Don't pretend to be shocked. Do you think you're holy? You were out at night. No good girl would be walking the streets this late." The man laughed scornfully.

"Please," Adila begged. "You knew I was lost. Please don't do this."

"Then we'll do it quick, and I'll release you."

"Are you crazy? I'm a virgin," Adila cried. "Don't do this."

The man changed his approach by saying that men get ill if they can't have sex. "Anyway, I don't want to rape you. I'll just hug you," he added, grabbing her and trying to take her clothes off.

Adila had no idea how to get out of the situation. She started to scream, but then he got angry and shouted back that if she made a noise many other men would come and rape her. Holding her down, he growled, "So I lied to you. I brought you here so I could have you. This field belongs to my gangster friends. We bring women here to rape and then kill them."

Adila inwardly cried out to God for help. As she did, the Holy Spirit came upon her and she forced him away, putting her hand on his head and praying loudly in tongues.

The man jumped back as if scalded. His body twitched as from an electric shock. "Stop," he said to my sister. "I didn't touch you. Stop praying!"

But when she did stop praying, his demeanor changed again. "Are you finished?" He roughly pushed her to the wet ground. "Let's do this."

Adila could have given up at that point, but she didn't. There was fight left in her. Again she put her hands on his head and resumed praying in the Spirit, more loudly than before, rebuking the spirit of lust in him. She saw the demonic look in his eyes and knew what she was dealing with.

Tears streamed down her cheeks as the Holy Spirit interceded. She fought both spiritually and physically.

Just then she felt God give her a word of knowledge.

"You know the shame this will bring me?" she pointedly demanded through her tears. "What if it happened to your sister?"

Her words struck him like hammer blows. Almost instantly he completely changed; even his eyes were different.

Adila knew God brought repentance and deliverance. Virginity and purity are very significant in our culture. On the wedding night a bride and groom consummate their marriage on a white sheet. The groom will then show the blood from the broken hymen to the guests to prove his wife was a virgin. There is real shame attached to a girl who is thought not to be a virgin, and she will have trouble finding a husband.

The man jumped back as if scalded. His body twitched as from an electric shock.

"I'm sorry," the man said meekly. "I will take you to church."

> **Adila cried tears of joy and relief. The Lord had protected and delivered her.**

Amazed at the miraculous turnaround, Adila cried tears of joy and relief. The Lord had protected and delivered her.

As they walked back out of the deserted area, seven other gang members arrived. Jeering, they laughed and wolf-whistled as they saw my sister.

Adila froze. What would happen now?

"Hey," one shouted. "You brought us a new girl."

"Yeah," the others agreed. "Let's try her out. Who goes first?"

"Get back!" the man snapped, now as fierce in Adila's defense as he had been enraged with lust before. "This is my girlfriend. You can't have her!" Quickly he escorted Adila out of the field.

> **God showed her He was able to protect her. In fact, we both were amazed anew at God's caring for women.**

The fear of the Lord had come upon him, and he protected her. The Lord had turned what was meant for evil into good. The man respectfully accompanied her all the way to church, telling her to never walk alone at night again.

Adila still shook when she told me the story. God showed her He was able to protect her. In fact, we both were amazed anew at God's caring for women.

The God of love treats women as precious in His sight. He defends the weak.

He is also the God of transformation. Later, the man who had been enraged with lust and then defended Adila began coming to the church himself. Jesus started to change his heart and mind.

THE SEEDS GROW

Once I knew that Jesus was my Lord, that heaven was for real and that I was going there one day, I didn't want to go there alone.

Every day I prayed the Holy Spirit would speak to and soften the hearts of my family. I prayed in earnest for my mother, father, brothers and sisters.

The first opportunity appeared about a month after I recognized Jesus as Savior and Lord, who had paid the price for me with His precious blood. My sister Malika was seventeen, about three years older than me when I began to share my faith with her. She was talented and creative, studying dressmaking and clothing fashion with a professional designer who lived in our building.

Malika was a devout Muslim, strongly influenced by our father and by a religious friend of hers from school. It was Malika's own decision to wear the veil covering her hair and to perform all the religious acts of a pious Muslim woman.

In the book of 1 Corinthians Paul talks about watching seeds of faith sprout: "I planted the seed, Apollos watered it, but God has been making it grow" (3:6 NIV).

This was exactly what happened with Malika. Watching the *Jesus* film in the street had stirred her deeply. She saw that Jesus was a good man, and she told me she did not understand why He was killed. She knew He was innocent.

I invited her to tae kwon do, and since she was interested in self-defense, she joined me on several occasions. She heard the Gospel Alim preached, paying close attention to what he said, but never expressed her innermost thoughts.

Several weeks passed and at last Malika said she was open to attending church. She sat with our friend Gamila, since I sang in the choir.

As the service proceeded, I saw familiar emotions cross her face. She, too, was struck by fear at the sight of the cross hanging on the wall, but she reacted positively to the music and the sounds of praise. The lines and the frown smoothed away as love and peace flooded her soul, just as they had my own.

"We need to tell everyone. Everyone! This is too wonderful to keep to ourselves!"

When at last there was an invitation to come forward for prayer, Malika rose and moved toward the front while Gamila went along with her. The light of the Holy Spirit's presence infused my sister's face as she gave her life to the Lord.

When we had a chance to be seated together, Malika exclaimed: "Jesus is real!"

I hugged her, and tears trickled down my cheeks as I whispered fiercely, "I know!"

Smiling wider than I had ever seen her, my sister announced,

"We need to tell everyone. Everyone! This is too wonderful to keep to ourselves!"

I felt like my heart would burst with joy! Here was the answer to my prayer. Malika was the first of my family to also come to Jesus, but I was certain all the rest would follow. Malika agreed she was the down payment on the redemption of all we loved. We covenanted together to pray for each of the others.

From that day on Malika had a hunger for the things of God. When she witnessed the passion and love for Jesus displayed by a missionary in our church, she wanted it, too. She never missed a Sunday or Friday night prayer service, doing whatever she could to get to the church. Malika did not continue with tae kwon do, but it had been part of the "watering" of her faith that led her to Christ.

With the joy I felt at watching Malika's response to Jesus came great satisfaction that things were going to improve in our country and for our family. Three long years of war had imprinted hopelessness and fear onto our lives, but now the clouds began to lift.

As a church we prayed earnestly for the promise of 2 Chronicles 7:14 (NIV) to be realized:

"If my people, who are called by my name, will humble themselves and pray and seek my face and turn from their wicked ways, then I will hear from heaven, and I will forgive their sin and heal their land."

We prayed for the war to end, for our families and friends to come to know Jesus and for our government to ensure peace and freedom for all of us.

Every Friday night we would worship and pray through many dark hours, begging God to have mercy on our nation. It was hard for me to attend these gatherings, though I hated to miss one ever.

I would sneak out of our apartment and run all the way to the church—a hazardous journey every time. The dark streets were empty because of the curfew and the danger, so we were not supposed to be outside before sunrise and after sunset, but my desire to fill my life with God's presence drew me to Him. Each Friday night I was willing to deal with both threats that my pilgrimage presented: discovery by my parents, including the inevitable explosion that would follow, and the jeopardy to my safety each trip presented.

The Lord reminded me of His promise in 2 Timothy 1:7: "For God has not given us a spirit of fear, but of power and of love and of a sound mind" (NKJV). Fear departed from me.

Once while I was walking back from church, I was confronted with a pack of hungry big dogs. Fangs bared, the snarling animals moved toward me. I knew the stories of the dogs attacking and killing people. As soon as I heard their howls I began to pray for safety.

"Lord, I know the story of Daniel in the lions' den is true! I know that You shut the mouths of the lions and prevented Daniel from being harmed. I ask now that You will shut the mouths of these savage dogs."

The dogs kept their distance from me as if a wall of fire surrounded me. I continued safely home, confident that God was with me in the dangerous war-torn streets of my city.

Often I tried to walk in a manly way and borrowed my brother's oversized coat and cap to disguise that I was a woman. I doubt I fooled anyone, but it made me feel less vulnerable. Again, thanks to the way Malika gave her heart to the Lord, as did Gamila, I was no longer alone. We went to Friday night services together.

The prayer times were so powerful. The arrival of the Holy Spirit's power was accompanied by wonderful signs. People laughed with joy of the Lord. They acted almost drunk with the power of the Lord's presence, just like at the time of the first

Pentecost. Many were healed and others delivered of demons as they worshiped.

One week's worship time reenacted another part of that first Pentecost:

> When the day of Pentecost came, they were all together in one place. Suddenly a sound like the blowing of a violent wind came from heaven and filled the whole house where they were sitting. They saw what seemed to be tongues of fire that separated and came to rest on each of them. All of them were filled with the Holy Spirit and began to speak in other tongues as the Spirit enabled them.
>
> Acts 2:1–4 NIV

I arrived just after it had happened but was in awe as people described the power of God. The Holy Spirit had come like a rushing wind, they said, so powerful that the windows cracked and broke! Members of the congregation fell prostrate on the floor in the presence of a mighty God, weeping in repentance and praying with renewed fervor for our country. I looked around and saw that the descriptions were all true.

My sister Malika was home all the time I was coming and going to the church during the three days of fasting, so I reported to her what was going on.

A Different Kind of New Year

The first New Year after I became a Christian was a very special time. It was a custom in my church to fast and pray during the holiday.

While I had fasted before as a Muslim, the Ramadan fasts only meant not eating and drinking until after sunset. This time of fasting meant that for three days I ate nothing and drank nothing but water, while the church read the entire New

Testament completely through. The readings were punctuated by prayer and worship.

Many of the worshipers slept in the church for those three days, but Malika and I had to be home to prevent our parents from asking too many questions. Still, I was grateful for all the times we were able to be there.

Fasting concentrated my attention on the things of God. I asked God what He wanted me to fast for and two great desires became very clear: First, the Lord was asking me to fast for my family and their salvation. I desperately wanted the rest of them to know the Lord. And second, I wanted to share in the heavenly language that some call "speaking in tongues":

> Now there are varieties of gifts, but the same Spirit. And there are varieties of ministries, and the same Lord. There are varieties of effects, but the same God who works all things in all persons. But to each one is given the manifestation of the Spirit for the common good. For to one is given the word of wisdom through the Spirit, and to another the word of knowledge according to the same Spirit; to another faith by the same Spirit, and to another gifts of healing by the one Spirit, and to another the effecting of miracles, and to another prophecy, and to another the distinguishing of spirits, to another various kinds of tongues, and to another the interpretation of tongues.
>
> 1 Corinthians 12:4–10

A visiting speaker invited those who wanted to receive the gift of heavenly language to come forward for prayer. When she put her hand on my forehead, I felt heat, as if I were being consumed with fire from head to toes. I started shouting "Hallelujah!" and then new, unknown words flowed out of my mouth. I was so happy I had received this gift and would speak and sing in heavenly language at every opportunity, especially when I was out on the streets and praying for safety. I was overwhelmed with the joy of the Lord, as never before. During that time, my sacrifice of food brought me closer to God.

I was also filled with the fruit of the Holy Spirit as described in Galatians 5:22–23: love, joy, peace, patience, kindness, goodness, faithfulness, gentleness and self-control. As I continue to be filled with the Holy Spirit, He fills me continually with His gifts and fruit.

The Celebration Banquet

At the end of the fast I felt the Lord prompt me to invite Adila to the celebration banquet.

I loved her so much and longed for her to know God's love for her. I heard the Lord tell me clearly: "This is the right place and right time."

To a Muslim the very word *church* can be disturbing and create resistance. Adila would not have come if I had spelled out that it was a church event, so I said she was invited to come to a party with me and my tae kwon do friends. "It'll be fun," I urged her. "We'll have delicious food and dancing but don't ask me anything else. It's a surprise."

Dancing is also part of our culture and an important part of the way we express joy. Celebrations like birthdays and weddings are always accompanied by dancing and singing. Adila and I had grown up attending dance classes at very young ages and excelled at it. But there had been very few opportunities to dance for several years.

The combination of dancing and generous provision of food in the midst of the deprivations of war was too much for Adila to resist. "I'll come," she agreed.

When we arrived at the banquet, we were greeted warmly by my pastor. "And this is your sister? Welcome! I'm so glad you can join us. Samaa has told us so much about you. Lots of us have been looking forward to meeting you. Please, let me introduce you."

Hospitality is also very important in Middle-Eastern culture. The host always serves his guests to make them feel like royalty, kings and queens. My pastor did the same for my sister and she felt honored.

He whisked Adila away into the crowd. I noticed by my sister's expression how happy she was to see so many young people enjoying themselves.

> Adila rose from the table and gave her plate of food to the man. "I'm not really that hungry," she said. "Why don't you take mine?"

My pastor, with support from some American churches, had been able to get food for the banquet. We were given lamb and other treats—a big deal after the years of near-starvation. Then, too, I knew the delight on her face mirrored my own at the sight of the platters of savory, fragrant dishes. They even had lamb kebab, our favorite dish.

As Adila and I sat down to enjoy our meal together, a homeless man appeared at the doorway. He was not part of the church, but it was clear he was needy and hungry.

Without announcing what she was about to do, Adila rose from the table and gave her plate of food to the man. "I'm not really that hungry," she said. "Why don't you take mine?"

It was ironic that it had been hearing about the food at the banquet that had convinced my sister to come, and now she was giving hers away.

The pastor, seated nearby, leaned toward me and whispered, "Your sister is very close to the Kingdom."

After supper we danced our national dance. We laughed and celebrated being alive and having hope.

Adila joined in the festivities without hesitation. "Thank you so much for asking me and encouraging me to come," she said. "This is the most fun I've had in a long time."

A time of prayer and worship followed the dancing. When these Christians prayed, they prayed loud! My sister watched in awe as they cried out to Jesus, weeping for those who didn't yet know Him. Others laughed and shook as the joy of the Lord came upon them. I could tell my sister loved the worship but did not understand the manifestations of the Holy Spirit. Again she peered at the cross at the front of the room, and her expression grew fearful. Little by little I explained what was happening, who Jesus was, and she began to feel less nervous.

After the banquet I gave Adila a tract explaining the Gospel, and she prayed the prayer of repentance.

Changed Hearts

The following Sunday Adila agreed to come with Malika and me. I was ecstatic. It had only been a few months, and now two of my sisters were coming to church with me! I praised God for His power in changing their hearts.

When we arrived and sat through the service, Adila was amazed. "This isn't what I expected," she said.

All her fears were unfounded as she, too, was overwhelmed by the love of the people and the love of God. When she was prayed for, she was delivered from her fear of death and had no more nightmares after this time. This was significant since, as a child, she had been tormented by nightmares with evil images and snakes.

I invited her to tae kwon do as well. She came to check it out but preferred the church meeting. One Friday night prayer time Adila was touched by the passion of my friend Mustafa, meaning "Chosen One," when she saw him worshiping God on his knees, hands raised into the air in total surrender. Adila wanted to know God like he did.

Later Mustafa left to go to another country to find work, and Adila and I would visit his father, who was partially sighted and wore thick glasses. As we prayed for him, a miracle happened—his eyesight was completely restored. He hugged us, tears streaming down his face as we all praised Jesus together.

Malika, Adila and I did not own a Bible of our own, just the New Testaments we had been given at church. We longed for a full Bible, but it was still not translated into our language. In the end it was a friend from church, Fadil, meaning "Virtuous, generous," who gave Adila her first Bible. I was both excited for her and also swept with longing. I wanted to have my own Bible, too, more than anything, but it seemed impossible to get one.

"My dream is to have a Bible."

"My dream is to have a Bible," I told Fadil when he gave Adila hers.

"Pray for it," he replied with a smile.

So I did. I prayed and fasted for three days that week, asking God for a Bible of my own.

The following Sunday I arrived at church, and Fadil wore a big smile. "I have something for you," he said, handing me a package.

Inside was a beautiful Bible. I was ecstatic! I had no idea how he had procured it, but it was such a precious gift. I hugged it close to my heart, thanking him profusely. I started reading and memorizing verses immediately. I couldn't get enough of it, avidly poring over the pages at every chance I got. I understood the verse in Matthew 4:4: "Man shall not live on bread alone, but on every word that comes from the mouth of God" (NIV).

After I read all 66 books of the Bible, especially the gospels, the Holy Spirit revealed to me that Jesus is the God-Man. In the incarnation, God became a Man and took on flesh. Because He is the great Creator God, all things are possible with Him. Thus, Jesus Christ is both fully God and fully Man.

As I searched the Bible, I found a gem—the revelation that it is all about Jesus. The Old Testament is the prophecy about the coming Messiah. And the New Testament is the fulfillment of that promise. The Messiah came the first time to save the world, and He will come the second time for His Bride, the Church.

As a woman, I searched out the life of women in the Bible, and I had a revelation about how the Lord had used weak women:

- Eve sinned, but her seed crushed Satan.
- Sarah, by faith, received her promised son in her old age.
- Through Deborah, the Lord brought victory.
- Ruth was a Gentile, but Jesus came from her line.
- Rahab was a harlot, but because she welcomed the spies, she and her family were not killed.
- Esther was born for such a time as this, and her people were redeemed by the hand of God through her boldness.
- Anna, a prophetess who ministered to the Lord by prayer and fasting, saw the Redeemer who brought redemption.
- Through her obedience Mary gave birth to Jesus, the Savior King.
- Mary of Bethany anointed Jesus' feet with expensive perfume, preparing Him for His burial.
- Mary Magdalene was the first person to see Jesus after His resurrection and before He returned to the Father.

Through those glimpses I understood how precious women are to Jesus.

I made sure my older brothers and sister didn't see me reading my new Bible, as it would have provoked them and made them angry.

In time I ended up with four Bibles in different languages and translations, and reading each of them helped my biblical understanding as well as my language studies. Since then I have read the Bible cover to cover at least thirty times. I try to read one book of the Bible per day. I enjoy reading the original Hebrew and Greek translations, as well.

Adila's Debt

The Lord had a plan to make each of us fit to work in His Kingdom. Learning His Word was one thing; living out His commands was another. There were times when the Lord's way of weaning us from things of this world was easy. Other times it was very difficult.

When Adila became a Christian, she had been smoking for over a year. She had been introduced to expensive cigars by some clients she worked for. "Bad company corrupts good character" (1 Corinthians 15:33 NIV). She wasn't a heavy smoker, but when she gave her heart to the Lord, she never smoked again. He instantly set her free from addiction to nicotine.

> The Lord had a plan to make each of us fit to work in His Kingdom.

In war people do what they can to make money. Adila was gifted with business, as are many people in the Middle East. We are traders, talented in bartering. Adila could sell anything. In her early teens she started selling clothes and whatever else she could acquire, which later led into selling gold, diamonds and other precious stones. She was initially very successful . . . until she was cheated and lost everything.

The whole episode started when she met a woman who said she wanted to buy all of Adila's stock, which was worth a huge amount of money. I was helping my sister in the business, so I went with her to the lady's home. The house was in a rich area of town, so we could tell she had money. Before we went any further in our business dealings with her, we told her about Jesus. She was touched and gave her heart to the Lord. She told us she did not have the money with her, but if we left all the clothes and jewelry, she would pay the next day.

Adila agreed. We trusted the lady since she had just asked Jesus into her heart. But we were too naïve. The next day Adila went back to find the woman was not there. We found out later that she was a harlot and did not live at that house. She had disappeared with all of my sister's stock. Adila lost everything and was now bankrupt. She had no way of repaying her huge debts.

My parents were mortified as debt collectors with guns came to our apartment, asking for my sister. They pulled her out in the street in full view of the neighbors, beating her and telling her much worse would come if she did not get the money to give to them.

My heart broke for my sister as I wiped the blood off her face from the beating. All I could do was pray. I had no money to help her repay what she owed. Our whole family was burdened emotionally with the debt, but Musa, who had the money, refused to give it to Adila, because he had heard from people in our community that she had become a Christian.

The experience broke my sister's heart, and she started to pray in earnest to Jesus. She was desperate, knowing she could be put in prison.

As Adila prayed, Jesus showed her that her success had taken her heart away from Him. Adila was making a lot of money and had started hanging around with bad company (see 1 Corinthians 15:33). Although she still believed, she was not following Jesus with her whole heart. God used the bankruptcy to focus Adila back on Himself.

Every morning I'd go to the church to pray at 5:00 a.m. and find Adila already there. She started getting more involved in every aspect of church life and joined a Bible study our friend Hakim led and an intercession group that I led. As she turned to God for help, He made a way.

Malika, who by that time was becoming a well-known dress-maker, was asked to make furnishings for the house of the man Adila owed money to. If she made all they asked, it would be accepted as part payment for the debt. Malika graciously agreed and spent long hours, often way into the night, sewing curtains and cushion covers.

With Malika's sewing, help from my father and income from a new job, Adila was able to pay back everything, and the interest she owed was waived. The sudden favor from these people was unbelievable. They were hard, violent men who had the power to put her in prison, but uncharacteristically they softened in their attitude toward my sister.

Carried by Angels

One night, after Friday night prayer, Adila, Malika and I decided to take a minibus from the church to our home. Since it was so dangerous to travel at night—especially for women—the minibus would drop us off at our houses. We were all laughing and joking as we bundled into the vehicle. As usual, before we left, someone asked who was going to pray for our journey. We always prayed before every journey, because each time we traveled, we took our lives in our hands.

"I will!" Adila, who was sitting in the front seat, replied. "Lord, bless our way," she prayed. "We plead the blood of Jesus over this car and our lives. Bring Your angels to protect us. We declare Psalm 91 over this journey—that whoever dwells in the shelter of the Most High will rest in the shadow of the

Almighty . . . that You will save us from the fowler's snare and from the deadly pestilence. You will cover us with Your feathers, and under Your wings we will find refuge; Your faithfulness will be our shield and rampart. We will not fear the terror of night, nor the arrow that flies by day, nor the pestilence that stalks in the darkness, nor the plague that destroys

> **The bus should have crashed. It was a miracle no one was hurt.**

at midday. A thousand may fall at our side, ten thousand at our right hand, but it will not come near us," she prayed.

Then, instead of ending her prayer, she continued to pray loudly and in heavenly language.

"Hey, Adila, relax. Stop being so spiritual," someone joked from the back.

We all laughed, but she didn't stop.

Suddenly our minibus hit something, and we went flying through the air. Everyone screamed, but the minibus seemed to be carried, as if by angels. We landed with only a bump, and one of the tires fell off as we skidded to a stop.

We were safe. The bus should have crashed. It was a miracle no one was hurt.

The driver and another guy got out to fix the tires, and we were soon on our way. We all sat in silence, taking in what had happened.

Shaken at our close shave, I put my hand on Adila's shoulder. Turning to me, she said, "I felt I had to pray hard, and that must have been why—God just saved us."

Later we found out that there had been a serious car accident at that spot earlier in the day, and people had died. I truly believe that Adila's spiritual sensitivity and prayers led God to spare our lives. Her spiritual sensitivity carried into other areas of her life, as well.

Adila had planned to go to university to study economics, but wondered if God was asking her to go to Bible school in a neighboring country instead. Our church had connections with a school in Eastern Europe, and we had been hearing all about it.

"Lord, if You want me to go to Bible school, please let me not be accepted to my university course," she prayed.

She took the exam, and although she is very intelligent, Adila did not get a place. She took this as a sign from the Lord that she was to go to Bible school. However, in order to go, she had to wait until she was nineteen. She enrolled in the late 1990s, and that year transformed her life. She felt so free being away from persecution, and the teachers and students loved her. Adila was at the top of her class and was asked to stay and work as a pastor with the people. After praying about the offer, she decided to say no. Instead she came back home to be with her family and serve her people, despite the threat of renewed persecution.

The Old Becomes New

About eight months after I became a Christian, the topic of baptism came up. One Sunday, as I was sitting in church with my two sisters, our pastor preached on Matthew 28:19–20 (NIV):

"Therefore go and make disciples of all nations, baptizing them in the name of the Father and of the Son and of the Holy Spirit, and teaching them to obey everything I have commanded you. And surely I am with you always, to the very end of the age."

I knew even Jesus was baptized (see Matthew 3:16), and I wanted to follow His example. This was not a light decision. There would be no turning back after baptism. I would be declaring to the world I was no longer a follower of the prophet Muhammad but a follower of Christ. For Muslims, such actions bear consequences, not only personally but to their entire lineage. A person is not simply an individual; he is the "father of" and the "son of." It is a tribal/community culture, very different from the individualistic West.

But I had found the pearl of great price, the salvation of my soul, and I was willing to give up everything for more of Jesus.

Our church held baptisms once a year in a lake outside of the city, and I, along with Gamila, Malika and Adila, signed up to be baptized. We had all been baptized by the Holy Spirit already and had our lives transformed. Now it was time to make a public declaration that "old things have passed away; behold, all things have become new" (2 Corinthians 5:17 NKJV).

The sun shone bright and warm on the Saturday of our baptism. It was about a year after my conversion. We met early in the church for worship and teaching on baptism. Then about two hundred friends and their family members drove in hired buses for an hour into the mountains. We arrived at a beautiful lake, nestled beneath the high peaks, the shore dotted with junipers. I breathed in the fresh air, and my heart raced with excitement at what I was about to do. Everyone praised God by the banks of the lake before our pastor and tae kwon do coach waded into the cool, clear water. Those who were to be baptized lined up and went into the water one at a time, dressed in white robes given to us by the church over our swimming suits.

My turn came, and I walked into the water.

"Do you, Samaa, repent of your sins and turn to Christ?" my pastor asked.

"I do," I solemnly replied.

I knew I was dying to the old me, and as I died with Christ, I was being made alive in Him.

"Then I baptize you in the name of the Father, the Son and the Holy Spirit," he said, putting his hand on my head and pushing me down into the water.

I was full of joy as I came up out of the water. I raised my hands high, and laughter burst out of me. I shouted out my praise to Jesus as the water dripped off my face. Everyone clapped and cheered. The atmosphere was a huge celebration, just like when a baby is born.

Adila, Malika and Gamila were also baptized. We spent the rest of the day eating delicious watermelon and lamb kebab, cooked over an open fire. My sisters and I then swam with our friends in the lake. It was such a joyous day, with the pain and horrors of the war momentarily forgotten or at least put to the back of our minds.

Community Shunning

It didn't take long before our neighbors were talking about what my sisters and I had done—not only in becoming Christians but being baptized. We were ignored in the street by longtime acquaintances and had stones thrown at us.

Our relatives also stopped visiting. This was hardest on my mother. She cried constantly. Because of our baptisms, the whole family was tarred with the same brush. We were now the infidel.

The elders at the mosque close to our house complained to my father about me, saying I was a bad example to the young people. They pressured my father to discipline us. "If you don't, we will," they threatened, meaning they would kill us . . . me especially.

> **Such boldness had come over me that I started to use every opportunity to share God's love.**

Despite this treatment, such boldness had come over me that I started to use every opportunity to share God's love. I even preached to Musa's friends. They griped to him about me, ridiculing and threatening him about his beloved sister, which was humiliating for him.

I knew they could kill me, but I learned to live the words of Matthew 10:28 (NIV):

"Do not be afraid of those who kill the body but cannot kill the soul. Rather, be afraid of the One who can destroy both soul and body in hell."

Our community—neighbors, relatives, everyone—shunned us. But it did not stop me from proclaiming my faith in Jesus.

Persecution

The happiness of our baptisms, and the memory of the sun-filled day, as well as the transformations I saw in my sisters, were in sharp contrast to the darkness that followed. Later I was struck by the realization that Jesus was taken into the desert after His baptism and was attacked by the devil. After my baptism, it was as if all hell broke loose, and I began to be persecuted by my own family for my faith.

My sisters and I each had been given a certificate of baptism. We proudly pasted them on the walls of our rooms. When my older brother Musa saw the certificates, he ripped them off the wall in a rage and stormed into the living room where we were sitting.

"What is this? Have you become Christians?" he demanded of my sisters and me.

"I have been baptized," I said to him, not wanting to hide the truth from the brother who had sacrificed for me and for whom I prayed daily.

He knew we had been going to church but didn't think we were serious about our new faith. He and the rest of my family had heard people in the community complain that we were now Christians, as we were evangelizing our friends and neighbors, but they assumed it was a fad and we would get over it and go back to being good Muslims soon enough. The baptism showed our decision was far from temporary and that we were fully committed to Christ.

Getting up and moving toward him, I gently tried to explain that I had met with the God of love, but my words infuriated him.

"Who is your mother? Who is your father? Who are your ancestors? They are *Muslim*, and *you* are Muslim. Do you want all of our family to become followers of Christ? Including *me?*" he asked incredulously, shaking with anger.

"Yes, not only you and our family, but I want the whole world to be saved and to know the truth because the truth sets you free," I replied, my eyes filling with tears as I saw his temper rising. "Jesus loves you; He died for you. He is the way, the truth and the life. My everything," I went on boldly. "He is not only a prophet but the Son of God."

Musa's hand shot out and slapped me across the face.

My own hand went instinctively to my red cheek. I was so shocked that he had hit me. I was his favorite sister, and he had spent his life protecting me. I could not fathom how he could attack me in such anger.

He swiftly grabbed my shoulders and threw me to the ground, hitting and punching me, letting all his anger and frustration out. My brother was strong and a trained boxer. He almost knocked me out with a punch. I cried out in pain. This was the first time I had been beaten by a family member, and I thought he was going to kill me.

But in the midst of the beating, I heard a still, small voice in my head: *"If someone slaps you on one cheek, turn to him the other also"* (Luke 6:29 NIV). I knew I could not fight back or use my tae kwon do or karate skills. So I just took the beating, and as I prayed, Matthew 5:10–12 came to mind:

> "Blessed are those who are persecuted because of righteousness, for theirs is the kingdom of heaven. Blessed are you when people insult you, persecute you and falsely say all kinds of evil against you because of me. Rejoice and be glad, because great is your

reward in heaven, for in the same way they persecuted the prophets who were before you."

NIV

As the Word of God comforted me, I was able to accept his beatings. My sisters had tried to intervene, but they were hit, too. I knew we were sharing in Christ's suffering, and because of that, I understood that we would also share His joy. Each time my brother punched me, I would say, "Jesus loves you!" This made Musa spit on me in disgust.

When the beating was over, I lay nearly lifeless on the ground,

The Word of God comforted me.

my body covered in bruises, blood trickling from my nose and tears spilling from my eyes. I felt as if my heart was breaking into a thousand pieces, but at the same time I felt the presence of the Comforter with me, giving me peace.

My other two sisters were also beaten, and they, too, did not fight back. I was the worst off as Musa saw me as the initiator, the recruiter. It was because of me that the others were now traitors to Islam and our family.

"You are not my sisters," he snarled, his anger eventually spent.

Yet all along I knew Musa's rage was motivated by his love for me. His heart was breaking to think that I had been so deceived. I had made the whole family unclean by my actions. However, I was no longer ruled by fear. I longed for my friends and family to experience the new life I had found.

When Musa attacked me, my father was not home, only Mama. Since in Muslim culture the man is the head of the family and has the authority, she could do nothing to stop Musa. She sat in the next room and cried, praying to Allah that we would stop going to church so we would not get hurt anymore.

Later, when Papa returned home with my oldest brother, Suleyman, he heard what we had done. He was angry but also brokenhearted by our actions. "You are my baby daughter. *How* could you do this?" he asked.

In Islam my father would be justified in killing us. It would be an honor killing as we lived in a shame culture and the only way to remove shame was by death. Leaving the Muslim faith and becoming a Christian is the worst kind of shame imaginable.

"Jesus is the only way, Papa, and He loves you," I replied.

Anger rose in my father and my brothers who were with him when I said that.

"You are not my daughter, unless you deny Jesus. You will only live if you return to Islam!"

"Papa, I cannot." Tears rolled down my already swollen cheeks.

"You will renounce Him, or I will disown you!" screamed my father, rushing toward me along with my brothers. His rough hands grabbed my neck to strangle me. "You have to return to being a Muslim because you were born Muslim; you have no choice but to die Muslim!"

As the breath was being squeezed out of me, two verses came to my mind:

> "Whoever acknowledges me before others, I will also acknowledge before my Father in heaven. But whoever disowns me before others, I will disown before my Father in heaven."
>
> Matthew 10:32–33 NIV

> Then he said to them all: "Whoever wants to be my disciple must deny themselves and take up their cross daily and follow me. For whoever wants to save their life will lose it, but whoever loses their life for me will save it. What good is it for someone to gain the whole world, and yet lose or forfeit their very self? Whoever is ashamed of me and my words, the Son of Man will

FACE to FACE with JESUS

be ashamed of them when he comes in his glory and in the glory
of the Father and of the holy angels."

Luke 9:23–26 NIV

"I will never renounce Jesus. No Jesus, no life. He is faithful
unto death for me, and I will be faithful unto death for Him,"
I choked, gasping for breath.

"You are foolishly *crazy*," he yelled, so frustrated at what
he saw as my stubbornness. His hands gripped tighter around
my neck.

> **"No Jesus, no life. He is faithful unto death for me, and I will be faithful unto death for Him."**

"Yes, crazy for Jesus. I will waste
my life for Him," I whispered.

Then I passed out.

I came around still lying where I
had fallen. I was all alone.

My father had left me beaten
and bruised on the ground, but he
did not kill me. When I passed out, they thought I was dead
and in terror left me.

With the last of my strength I crawled to my room with my
sisters. Lying on the bed, I silently cried out to God for help. I
had only known the love and favor of my family while growing
up. Now, for the first time, I was experiencing violent persecution from those I loved most, and it broke my heart. Like Joseph
in the Bible (see Genesis 50:19–20), my brothers had betrayed
me, but I trusted God to turn every evil to good. I held tightly
to the promise of Romans 8:28: "And we know that God causes
all things to work together for good to those who love God, to
those who are called according to *His* purpose."

Hours went by, and we were not allowed to leave our room.
The day seemed to last forever. Life had become very hard since
following Christ. I knew it was the narrow path and could cost
me my life, but Jesus was worth it. Even though I had been

152

beaten to the point of passing out, my love for Jesus was never shaken.

I never judged or hated my father and brother for what they did. I forgave them, and by the mercy and grace of God I did not have any bitterness against them. I understood it was because of their great love for me that they were trying to stop me from going down what they thought was the wrong path. I felt the Holy Spirit show me that if I tried to fight for myself, His hands would be tied, but if I let go and trusted Him, He would protect me. The Word of God was my comfort, and two verses helped me at that time: "Be still, and know that I am God" (Psalm 46:10 NIV) and "Do not be afraid. Stand still, and see the salvation of the LORD" (Exodus 14:13 NKJV). That's why, even while my father and brother were beating me, I continued to say, "I love you; Jesus loves you." They could not keep me quiet.

Papa said that, if we ever tried to go to church again, we would be punished. He took my sisters' and my outdoor clothes and locked us in our rooms so we could not escape to go to church.

I knew he was serious, but I did not let the fear of death stop me.

My Escape to Church

The next day I waited until Papa and my brothers had gone out to find work before escaping.

I climbed over the balcony of our second-floor apartment and, holding on to the pipes, jumped to the ground floor. I could hardly see with both my eyes so swollen, but I put on sunglasses to cover them and hoped no one would notice.

I felt responsible for my sisters, who had been baptized with me. I needed to pray for guidance from the Holy Spirit and to get some encouragement and comfort to bring back to them. I prayed 2 Corinthians 1:3–4:

Blessed be the God and Father of our Lord Jesus Christ, the Father of mercies and God of all comfort, who comforts us in all our affliction so that we will be able to comfort those who are in any affliction with the comfort with which we ourselves are comforted by God.

Limping, and in pain, I made it to church. At that time it was open 24/7 for prayer and worship.

I opened the door and made my way up to the prayer room. As I walked in, I saw my pastor.

"Samaa, is that you?" he asked, concerned.

"Yes, it's me," I said weakly, tears falling down my cheeks.

"Why are you crying?" Then he gasped at the blue bruises on my arms and neck.

"I am not crying for physical pain, but I am crying as I don't want my family to be lost," I said before explaining all that had happened.

My pastor, who was like a spiritual father to me, had tears in his eyes as I told him how my family had beaten us.

Together we prayed and asked the Lord to speak.

"I feel this is a spiritual battle," my pastor said finally.

I was reminded of Ephesians 6:12 (NIV):

For our struggle is not against flesh and blood, but against the rulers, against the authorities, against the powers of this dark world and against the spiritual forces of evil in the heavenly realms.

I knew it was the devil and not my family who was the enemy. As Matthew 17:21 says, "This kind does not go out except by prayer and fasting" (NKJV).

I felt that I needed to fast for seven days and told my pastor. He said that if God was telling me to do that, then I had to obey, but that I must be careful. I didn't know how I was going to do it; I had never fasted for that long before. But God spoke to my heart: "My grace is sufficient for you, for power is perfected in weakness" (2 Corinthians 12:9).

His voice brought me peace. I was only fifteen years old. The most I had ever fasted was three days, and it hadn't been easy. I didn't know how I would fast for a whole week, but I knew God would help me, and I had to obey. I like food, but I love Jesus more. My hunger for Him was more than my hunger for food.

My tae kwon do coach, Johnny, happened to be at church while I was there and he drove me home, encouraging and praying for me on the way. I got back just before my father and brothers returned.

I now had renewed hope as I told Adila and Malika what had happened. They decided to fast for three days, while I needed to be obedient and fast for a week.

For those seven days I prayed day and night and I felt God's presence so intensely that one hour felt like five minutes. I didn't notice that I was not eating food, because it was as if I was feasting with Him. Each day, when my father and brothers had left the house, I would sneak out and go back to church.

Mama knew I escaped, but she didn't tell Papa. She was terrified of what would happen to me if she did.

At church we had a prayer room made from stones and rocks. It was my secret place, and I would spend hours there in God's presence praying in the heavenly language and

> **For those seven days I prayed day and night and I felt God's presence so intensely that one hour felt like five minutes.**

in my natural language, able to express myself as loudly as I wanted. My faith was built up by hearing the Word (see Romans 10:17) and by worshiping and singing to Jesus.

While I was fasting and praying, I read and meditated on Scripture, such as Joshua 24:15, "But as for me and my house, we will serve the LORD," and Acts 16:31, "Believe in the Lord Jesus, and you will be saved, you and your household."

I claimed them as promises and spoke them out as praises. I praised God for the day my whole household would be saved.

After spending hours at church I would make my way home, always getting there just before my father and brothers. Over the seven days that I had been praying, God spoke to me about each one of my family.

The Lord said that Musa was like Saul in the New Testament, who zealously persecuted those who followed Christ. But Saul eventually had an encounter with Jesus on the road to Damascus, and from that day on surrendered his life to follow Jesus. Saul's name was changed by God, and he was then called Paul. I felt God say, "As zealous as Musa is for Islam, he will one day be more zealous for Christ." And the Lord confirmed it through a friend, who prophesied the same thing. And Suleyman would be like Simon Peter, the Rock, and my dad would be like Moses and encounter the living God in his later days.

I was drawn closer to the Lord as I prayed for my brothers and Papa. As Jesus says in Matthew 5:44, "Pray for those who persecute you." When I followed Jesus' command, I could hear God more clearly, and I harbored no bitterness or unforgiveness.

The fourth day my mother realized I was not eating, even though I had tried to hide it.

"Samaa, have some food," she urged. She was worried for me after the beating, and as I was the youngest, she always spoiled me, giving me extra-special meals and making sure I was well fed.

"I can't, Mama."

"Are you fasting?" she asked outright.

I could not lie. "Yes, Mama, I am."

"Why are you fasting, my baby? You were forced to go without food in the war. Now is the time to eat. You need to make up for all the nutrients you lost in the fighting," she insisted, putting a plate of fruit in front of me.

When I did not give in and eat the food she was offering, Mama told me she would fast with me.

"Mama, I am fasting in obedience to God, so I have the help of the Holy Spirit. You can't do it in your own strength," I said.

She ignored me and started to fast as well, but after three days she became very ill and fainted. A doctor was called to our home, and she had to be put on a drip to get fluids back in her body as she was badly dehydrated.

"What have you done to our mother?" Musa accused when he came home.

At that time I understood even more that we cannot do anything without God. Even fasting needs the grace of God. My heart was breaking as I prayed for Mama. She was very weak from the fast but thankfully made a full recovery.

After seven days of fasting, I knew there had been a breakthrough. My father and brothers calmed down. They were so busy trying to find work, they seemed to have forgotten all about us. But I'm convinced God blinded their eyes.

It was a breakthrough for me personally to complete my seven-day fast.

Acts 13:2 says the disciples "ministered to the Lord and fasted." For me, also, fasting became a way of life, a form of worship to the King. Once I had the breakthrough, I did more fasts. Sometimes they were two days or three days. Other times they were seven days, ten days, or 21 days. Each time I fasted it was in obedience to specific directions from the Lord, and the Holy Spirit gave me the grace to go without food. Without His help I could not have fasted a meal on my own strength. I loved to fast because of the intimacy with Jesus it brought.

15

A BOLD FAITH

As the leaves of the trees were turning that fall after our water baptism, Adila, Malika and I went on a three-day retreat in the mountains with our church. As the bus wound up the narrow road, it seemed to me that there was no war or sorrow. The sky was bright blue above the towering mountain peaks, and the air smelled clear and fresh.

The retreat was part of an international Christian renewal movement. Someone was assigned to pray for each candidate— girls for girls and boys for boys. For three months previously that person had prayed, fasted and prepared for his or her guest.

In order to go on the retreat, we told our family that we were going camping with tae kwon do friends to get more training in the high mountains. This was true, but we didn't mention that the trip was with our church and that it was also spiritual training.

I was only fifteen at the time. To be able to go on the retreat you had to be sixteen, but I had asked a favor from my pastor.

I was so eager to go and draw close to God that I fasted and prayed and eventually he relented. I knew it was God who had changed his heart.

The retreat was a gift to my sisters and me. The time we spent with the 400–500 participants in the beautiful, majestic mountains was filled with teaching about God's love, and we encountered Jesus in a powerful way. I cried as the woman assigned to me washed my feet tenderly, just as Jesus had washed the feet of His disciples. In that profound moment I glimpsed the humility and servant-heartedness of Jesus in her as she served me. My heart swelled with love for my Lord.

We knew our own family loved us deeply, but a distance had been created between them and us because of our new faith in Jesus and the rejection of our inherited faith.

My sisters and I were now part of a loving, accepting church family. We experienced firsthand the words of Matthew 19:29: "Everyone who has left houses or brothers or sisters or father or mother . . . for my sake will receive a hundred times as much and will inherit eternal life" (NIV).

I felt Jesus was saying that He saw the cost of our faithfulness and that He recognized the sacrifice we were making to follow Him. My heart still yearned for all my family to be saved. I prayed for that miracle of Christ's revelation to my loved ones many times a day. I believed that He heard and would answer those prayers.

Iman's Decision

Shortly after we came back from the retreat, my sister Iman became a Christian. At twenty, she was five years older than me, and I had been praying and fasting for her over the last year. She would listen as I shared little bits of my experience of Jesus but never showed much interest.

We had a retreat reunion in a huge circus tent the church rented out. Hundreds of us worshiped together. I invited Iman, not thinking she would say yes, since she was a Muslim, practicing Islam, but she did.

In the worship she was touched by the Holy Spirit and started to cry.

When the pastor asked if anyone wanted prayer, I whispered, "If you want to go forward, I will go with you."

Iman gazed up front. As the pastor placed his hand on each person's forehead, many of them fell to the ground. She lowered her chin and replied, "I can't. I'm too shy. If I fall down, I would be embarrassed. Everyone would be looking at me. I don't want to get my clothes dirty. . . ." The excuses tumbled out.

Jesus met with my sister as she lay in His presence.

I was sure she wanted to go forward, but I also knew she wouldn't go without my encouragement. "I'll come with you." I smiled and took her hand.

We walked forward together, arm in arm. When the power of God touched Iman, she couldn't stay standing. As she let go, all her fears were washed away, and she was filled with joy. She could not stop weeping. Jesus met with my sister as she lay in His presence.

The following Sunday she came to church and sat on the third row back, next to two old ladies. Adila, Malika and I were in the choir, so we couldn't sit with her. As we worshiped, she worshiped, too, with all her heart. Where once she was shy, she now praised Jesus with abandon, no longer worried what people would think. When the newcomers were welcomed, she stood to be sung to by the congregation.

"We greet you in the name of Jesus Christ," they sang.

When the song ended, one of the older ladies turned to her and said, "I never would have guessed you are a newcomer. You worship as if you are a believer!"

After the service I told her she should join the choir as she was a beautiful soprano.

"Oh, my voice isn't good enough!" She laughed.

"You're wrong about that," I corrected, "but Jesus isn't concerned with your voice. He looks at the heart, and you have the heart of a worshiper like King David in the Bible. God has anointed you to worship Him in spirit and in truth."

Iman eventually agreed and was accepted into the choir to sing as a soprano.

A Courageous Faith

I loved to see how God was transforming my sister. It was like watching a butterfly come out of a chrysalis. She came alive with joy. Iman was so excited about Jesus that, with a new boldness, she would talk about Him at every opportunity.

At that time she was working as an accountant for a car manufacturer. She had taken over a pregnant co-worker's job as cashier and was so conscientious that one Saturday she went into work to count the money for the staff salaries so it would be ready for Monday morning. It was so cold in her office that she took the money to the guards' room, where there was a small heater. Together with the two guards she sat in the warmth and started to count the money—it was the equivalent of almost 100,000 U.S. dollars. At the same time she began to share the Gospel with the men as she worked.

Suddenly the slamming of a door made her look up. Her pulse raced as she looked through the glass window of the guards' room. Four gangsters with guns barged into the building.

"Lord, please protect us," she prayed, hiding the money under the cushion of the chair she was sitting on.

The men burst through the office door and pointed their guns at the guards and my sister.

"We want all your money! Give it to us, and you might not die," shouted one of the men, looking straight at Iman.

Before she could reply, out of fear one of the guards betrayed her. "Look at her—she is a traitor to the faith. She was Muslim and has now become a Christian."

At first she was very afraid, but as she silently prayed, the Lord gave her peace.

One of the gangsters peered closer at my sister and gestured at the earrings she wore that were in the shape of a cross.

"Is it true? Are you a Christian?" he asked gruffly.

"Yes!" she replied and boldly began to share the Gospel and the love of Jesus with them.

"Shut up, you infidel!" said one of the men, taking his gun and violently pressing the muzzle into her neck.

She was fervently speaking in tongues and binding the demonic work in the men.

"Lord, please protect us," she prayed.

"Hey, she isn't doing anything wrong. She only believes in God," said another gangster, trying to stand up for Iman.

But instead of helping the situation, the argument made the man with the gun even angrier. "Shut your mouth," he growled, then proceeded to tell Iman how he would murder her, slowly and painfully.

"If you kill me, I will go to heaven. But where will you go?" she asked, not affected by his threats. "Jesus is the Son of God, and He loves you and died for your sins. He made a way for you to go to heaven if you only repent and believe in Him."

Then all four men left the office to talk to their boss, who had been waiting outside. After a few minutes the boss, wearing a dark suit, came in to speak to Iman. "Renounce Jesus and come back to Islam, or we will kill you," he said matter-of-factly.

"I am not afraid to die, and I will never stop telling you that Jesus loves you," replied Iman.

The militia boss started interrogating her, asking how she had become a Christian.

"My sister told me about Jesus," Iman said.

"Then we will kill her and your whole family," he threatened.

"If you kill me, I will go to heaven. But where will you go?"

Bolstered by supernatural courage, Iman repeated again and again that Jesus loved them and that He is the only Savior.

In anger he put his pistol to her head, while another gangster pulled out a knife and put it to her throat. It seemed my sister was about to be killed.

Then, suddenly, the Holy Spirit gave Iman inspiration and also the Spirit of knowledge. In a strained voice, trying to ignore her throbbing cheek, she said calmly, "I thought this was Ramadan. It is supposed to be a holy month of prayer and fasting, and you are killing people?"

The crime boss looked at her, wavering in his decision. Slowly he lowered the gun and signaled for the gangster with the knife to move away. "We will come back after Ramadan to kill you. We will cut you into tiny pieces because you are a traitor to the faith," the bandit captain said before storming out of the office.

As the gangsters followed their chief, Iman breathed a prayer of thanks to the Lord that she was still alive and then rejoiced again, especially when she realized that the money was still safe under the cushion.

"Iman, you would be wise to return to Islam, if you want to stay alive," said her company director when he heard what had happened.

"I will never go back," she replied, knowing that God had saved her life.

The director asked her to stop evangelizing, but she insisted that she could not. She had found a love so wonderful that she could not keep it to herself; she had to share it.

From then on Iman had favor in her workplace, and she became much bolder. Everyone respected her for her bravery. She forgave the guard who betrayed her and was known as a woman of honesty and integrity.

I watched as the Lord strengthened my sisters in their faith. Iman had faced death, yet still remained faithful. I was so proud of her. Before my eyes my family was being transformed by the power of the Holy Spirit.

A New Opportunity

A year after Iman became a Christian, our pastor asked if anyone wanted to be a missionary. If they did, he suggested they go to Bible school.

"You want to be a missionary, don't you? You should go to Bible school!" I said to Iman.

"No way. I am only a new believer. I don't know anything," she replied, dismissing my suggestion.

"Well then, it's a perfect opportunity!"

"And I am not clever," she worried.

"The Lord will make you strong in your weakness. As you study the Word, He will give you the mind of Christ. Pray and fast and ask the Lord if He wants you to go. He will give you confirmation," I assured her.

She agreed to pray and decided to fast as well.

At the Friday night of prayer and worship God gave her a vision. She saw Jesus standing on the altar dressed in scarlet. In His hands was an open Bible. Then she saw our pastor in the vision; he, too, was dressed in red and had an open Bible in his hands. Even though they didn't speak, she knew what it meant. God was showing her it was time to study the Bible. She cried as she told me because she realized that God had a calling and plan for her life.

When Iman decided to leave her job in the late 1990s to go to the Bible school in Eastern Europe, her colleagues were all crying as they said good-bye to her. The love of God had shone through her, influencing her co-workers.

A year later the course finished, and Iman returned to our home city. She worked for the church—leading Bible studies, Sunday school, street evangelism and three cell groups.

16

SALVATION OF THE HOUSEHOLD

One summer in the late 1990s, a Christian medical mission came to my city. They used acupuncture to heal the sick, preached the Gospel and prayed for the patients. The Medical Mission advertised on national TV, and thousands came, even high-ranking officials.

There were many unwell in my country, mainly because the hospitals were not working well as a consequence of the war. The best doctors had left the country years before in a bid for safety.

The Medical Mission had an interesting history. Many years earlier an American doctor became paralyzed while serving in the military. Medical staff said he would never walk, so he became hopeless and depressed. His wife was a Christian, although he was not. She prayed for him continually, but instead of getting better, he got worse. He ended up living like a homeless man in a cave, dragging his body around with his arms.

While he was in this condition, in desperation he cried out to Jesus. The Lord gave him a revelation of how He would heal him through acupuncture. Miraculously the man got better and was able to walk. As a consequence he dedicated his life and his gift with acupuncture to the Lord. He used his skill to go on many mission trips, even treating sheiks in Saudi Arabia.

A special father/daughter friendship developed between one of the leaders of the Medical Mission and me. Dr. Kim, a man in his sixties, took special notice of me. He would bring me along to pray for patients with him and was touched when he saw how I cried with compassion for those in pain. He knew my family situation and was inspired by how much time I spent in prayer and worship.

Dr. Kim said that, because he had two sons but no daughters, he wanted me to be his daughter. He asked me to call him "Dad" or "Daddy." It was such a lonely time when I was being beaten and rejected by my family at home that this was a wonderful comfort.

Dr. Kim and the other missionaries brought the Medical Mission to my country every summer. God used acupuncture to heal and to save many Muslim friends and neighbors.

Dawud's Journey

During this time I was a translator for the doctors at another medical mission. There was a team of nearly twenty Christian doctors from America who were all experts in acupuncture. I worked with Dr. Kim and saw many miracles. The lame walked; the blind would begin to see. I watched how he, full of compassion, prayed for his patients. Dr. Kim was like an angel to the people he treated. I never guessed that one day he would treat me and save my life.

It was during the first medical mission that my brother Dawud, eight years older than me, came to Christ. When he was three years old, he had become deaf in his right ear. No one knew for sure what had caused it . . . whether it had been a loud noise that had burst his eardrum or an infection. He could only hear if you shouted, so he went to a school for those with hearing impairments.

I preached to my brother and gave him tracts with the Gospel message on them. One Friday night I had an idea. I asked him to walk me to church as it was dark, I was going alone and I had to take a heavy bag.

As a protective brother, he walked me there and carried the bag for me. When we arrived, I told him he might as well stay and see what it was like, then walk me back home after the service at 5:00 a.m., when it was still dark.

> **My brother Dawud, eight years older than me, came to Christ.**

"Samaa!" Dawud said in an annoyed tone. But I could tell he was only pretending since he stayed.

Dawud was touched by the worship and prayer, just as my sisters had been. There had been many miracles of deaf ears being healed at my church, and I told Dawud about this. His desire for healing brought him back, and he invited Jesus into his heart at one of the services after having an encounter with Jesus when he was prayed for.

Over the following months, he began to bring all his deaf friends to church. I had learned sign language to communicate with my brother, so I began to translate the sermons in sign language for his friends.

One of them was from the strictest Muslim country. He had been a soldier there but became deaf after an explosion. He loved coming to church, gave his heart to Jesus and later married a Christian girl.

Dawud was baptized in the lake outside our city with Iman two years after my salvation.

Healing for Mama

During another medical mission, to my great amazement and joy, my mother and brothers Suleyman and Musa agreed to receive treatment. It wasn't hard to convince them as they were sick and needed medical help, and the acupuncture was free.

Suleyman had tuberculosis, which he contracted in the war. My mother, who had a heart problem, was also suffering from headaches. Musa had pain in his back and legs due to an injury when he was in the army.

While they were in the line waiting to be treated, they were told about the God of love by friends from church. My family listened, and Mama's heart was touched. Then the team members laid hands on each person and prayed for them in Jesus' name. My mother and brothers did not mind this as they knew Jesus was a prophet and it is acceptable to be prayed for as a Muslim. Often patients would be healed then and there, but if they still needed treatment, they would then go in to have the acupuncture.

It was when my mother went to have treatment that she, too, became a follower of Christ. As she was waiting to have the acupuncture, Nuh came to talk to her. He was very well educated and had even been a Mullah before he became a Christian in the early 1990s. Now he and his brother-in-law, Yunus, meaning "Dove, the symbol for peace," were radical disciples for Christ.

After they told my mother about Jesus, the King of kings, she asked to accept Jesus in her heart. She was cured of her heart problem and headaches.

We had been praying for my family to have dreams and visions from Jesus. He had answered two weeks earlier when Jesus appeared to my mother in a dream. Clothed in beautiful white, He told her He would give her abundance and riches (see John 10:10). He also told her not to worry, but to cast all her cares on Him (see 1 Peter 5:7).

It was three years after my own salvation when Mama acknowledged Jesus as her Lord and Savior. She kept her newfound faith to herself, for fear of Papa's wrath, and it was very difficult for her to come to church. She only visited a couple of times during the following years.

But now she had peace. She prayed at home and would often ask us to pray for her.

Muqaddas's Challenge

About that time my sister Muqaddas, still a staunch Muslim, was going through a very hard time at work. We had been praying and fasting for her, but she had not been interested in hearing about Jesus. She told us we were crazy and should return to Islam.

Muqaddas was working as the finance officer at a university in our city. She was in charge of giving out the salaries for all employees. She was given a lot of responsibility at a very young age and was able to continue her work even during the war.

The university was next to an area that had been used for murdering people by the Opposition militia. A quarry there was turned into an open grave. Every morning the police would come to take away the new bodies. Muqaddas saw terrible things: Two men were stabbed right in front of her when she was going to work, and many times she was caught in a crossfire. She knew it was a miracle that she had escaped with her life.

After the war had ended, someone stole money from the salaries at the university. It looked like Muqaddas was going to be blamed as there were only three people who held a key to the safe—the director, a senior accountant and my sister. As Muqaddas was the youngest and the easiest target, she was taken to court and accused. She was desperate, because if she was found guilty, it would mean a prison sentence.

One evening she sat in our bedroom close to tears. The next day the judge was going to sum up the case and we would find out if Muqaddas had been found guilty. I knew I had to say something, but the only hope I could give her would be to turn to Jesus Christ, and I couldn't speak openly at home in case my father or brothers heard.

"Let's go outside and talk," I said gently. With my arm around her we walked downstairs and sat in the garden attached to our building. It was dusk and still warm. "Muqaddas," I began, "Jesus Christ is your Deliverer. Only He can help you in this situation. He is your only hope."

She was desperately anxious, so she let me pray for her. Just as we were about to go back inside, I gave her a challenge: "Ask Jesus to help you, and see what He does."

> **The only hope I could give her would be to turn to Jesus Christ.**

She agreed, and the next day came home with a huge smile. The court had found that the director and the senior accountant had stolen the money and conspired to blame Muqaddas. It was all out in the open, and they were sent to prison while Muqaddas was vindicated. She knew then that Jesus had helped her.

Muqaddas became a Christian. But she didn't commit her life fully until a few years later, when she went on a retreat in the mountains. At that point she became so passionate that she started preaching to our brother Suleyman. They were close in age and had been good friends growing up, but her decision to follow Christ created a rift between them.

"You are not my sister," Suleyman said in disgust. "You have become one of them—the infidel."

But Muqaddas did not give up.

Mubarak's Heartache

Five of my siblings were now attending services with me: Muqaddas, Dawud, Iman, Malika and Adila. My oldest brothers, Suleyman and Musa, and sister Mubarak were the ones who continued to persecute us, along with my father.

Mubarak was so angry she ripped up the New Testament I gave her and shouted that I was not her sister, that I was a traitor. I tried to explain, but her heart was closed.

Mubarak, born in the 1970s, had seen terrible things during the civil war because of her work as a policewoman.

Her close friend and co-worker was killed in a car accident. She was young and betrothed to a man but died before she could marry him. We went to her funeral and wept for this dear, lovely friend.

Mubarak also got bread to our family from the main factory that was close to her workplace. She risked her life multiple times, staying in line in spite of the snipers. Many people were shot, injured or killed. My sister witnessed death countless times, yet miraculously lived.

The building close to her police office was also bombed. Many were injured severely or killed. Others were brutally tortured, beaten and shot in front of her eyes. She couldn't help them, even if she'd wanted to. She'd been paralyzed with fear for her own life that they would see her and come after her. After that trauma, she started having nightmares.

Not long after the end of the war, Mubarak developed a bowel disease that meant she could not keep food down. She also suffered from a skin pigmentation problem, so the skin on her body was blotchy. Co-workers and people on the streets made fun of her because of this. She was so depressed and weak that she couldn't work anymore.

My Christian sisters and I simply continued to pray for her healing and salvation, waiting for God's timing and breakthrough. In the end it was her illness that led her to God. She was desperate for healing. My family had tried everything, from the doctors to the Imams and Mullah, but she was still so ill.

When the Medical Mission came to our city, I told Mubarak that Jesus could heal her. She agreed to

I told Mubarak that Jesus could heal her.

go to the mission. The acupuncture clinic was held on the third floor of our church building, but before patients had treatments, they were taken to a room on the first floor to hear the Gospel.

What touched Mubarak most was the compassion and love the doctors showed her. It was so different from the treatment she had received in the hospitals in our city, and a wall was broken down in her heart toward Christians.

Later Mubarak allowed me to pray with her, but it was not until three years later, through another friend sharing the Gospel with her, that she came to the Lord. Her physical healing came slowly, but her heart, which had been bitter and angry, was softened by the love of God. Mubarak was a new woman praying and praising Jesus Christ, her Lord and Savior, her Healer.

God was fulfilling Acts 16:31 in my family: "Believe in the Lord Jesus, and you will be saved, you and your household."

HEAVEN

In spite of daily danger in the world around me, in spite of my father's disapproval and my brother's persecution, I had never been so happy! The joy of the Lord was my strength, the strength of my sisters, one of my brothers and my mother! We shared a spiritual bond that transcended even that of our natural family ties. We lived each day in the awe and wonder of a real relationship with a God who is alive and who cares for every detail of our lives.

The fire of that joy spread, and many strangers came, seeking answers for their sorrows, just as we had done. No one was turned away. All were welcomed with the familiar love that had beckoned to my heart in the midst of a terrible civil war.

One Saturday I was praying till late in the night, standing in the gap and interceding with the Great Intercessor. Romans 8:34 tells us, "Christ Jesus is He who died, yes, rather who was raised, who is at the right hand of God, who also intercedes for us." The Spirit was groaning within me, and I felt a heavy burden of alert and urgency.

The next morning, Iman stood at the entrance of the church.

Four somber young men with grim expressions approached on Sunday morning. They were old enough that they had probably fought in the war. Who could know what horrible crimes they had committed in the name of Allah for one warring faction or another? By their pained looks they clearly harbored something terrible in their hearts. But Jesus, as Healer and Forgiver, can give even desperate men and women new beginnings.

She clasped their hands as they entered. "Welcome! Welcome, friends! Come in! Jesus loves you!"

Other members of the congregation spotted the newcomers and welcomed them with the same profuse and genuine love. Many brothers from the church, including our dear friend Wafa, made them their special project every Sunday for about two months as they sat among us and listened to the message of the Gospel. "Come in! We are so happy to have you here among us! Jesus loves you and so do we!"

We called Wafa the "Apostle Paul," because on outreach he'd been bitten by a poisonous snake but just shook it off and felt no effects from the poison. Even so, he was taken to the hospital.

The doctors were shocked he was still alive. "With this snake bite you should be dead within fifteen minutes!" they said.

Wafa's story was similar to the apostle Paul's in Acts 28:5 (NIV): "But Paul shook the snake off into the fire and suffered no ill effects."

The day before this particular Sunday, Wafa had taken all his friends from Bible school out to a meal as he wanted to bless them. Even though he was an only child to his parents, he was generous.

Little did he know it would be his last supper.

The Plot

The four young men watched us and plotted and waited for the right moment. When they were with us, they accepted our friendship. When they left each week, they discussed how we entered and departed the building and where four bombs could be planted to do the most damage. As they devised their plans, they constructed four weapons with instruction and materials from their Jihadist masters. They planted three bombs the day before, and a fourth was carried in by one of the men during service that Sunday.

Four bombs were set to explode fifteen minutes apart in order to kill the innocent and unsuspecting.

The first exploded in the auditorium.

The second, in the hall, miraculously did not explode.

The third bomb was beneath the stairwell and placed in the fire extinguisher cabinet where I spoke to Wafa and Sultan.

The fourth device was placed outside and meant to slaughter the remainder of us who were trying to help the wounded and dying. It didn't detonate either. Praise God!

I don't know if anyone would have survived if the second and fourth bombs would have exploded.

Explosion!

I was nearest to the third bomb, leaning against the fire extinguisher cabinet when it exploded. Wafa was decapitated in that instant. My body was burned and my head split open. Friends told me later they could see inside my skull.

Thrown ten feet into the air and smashed against the opposite wall, I called out to Jesus silently in my agony: "Jesus, help me!" And then, in that instant, my spirit left my body and I died.

> I know a man in Christ who fourteen years ago—whether in the body I do not know, or whether out of the body I do not know, God knows—such a one was caught up to the third heaven. And I know such a man—whether in the body or out of the

body I do not know, God knows—how he was caught up into Paradise and heard inexpressible words, which it is not lawful for a man to utter.

2 Corinthians 12:2–4 NKJV

When I opened my eyes I saw brilliant white light illuminating Jesus, the Son of Man, the Son of God. His face was brighter than the sun, and He was so glorious and transcending that I was blinded with unapproachable Light. Everything around me was bathed in golden light. I trembled in awe in His mighty presence, and the fear of the Lord descended upon me. Seeing the majesty and indescribable beauty of the Lord made me speechless. Yet every fiber of my being exclaimed, "Holy, holy, holy is the Lord God Almighty" as I worshiped the worthy Lamb of God.

With the weight of His glory, my trembling body fell face-down, prostrate at His feet. I was terrified, completely undone and aware that I was unclean. How could I stand in the presence of such a holy, awesome God (Isaiah 6:1–6; Revelation 4:8)?

At that moment I experienced Jesus' touch, and He said, "Do not be afraid." He reminded me that His precious blood was shed for me and had washed me as clean as white snow, making me holy and pure, because He loves me.

From him who is, and who was, and who is to come, and from the seven spirits before his throne, and from Jesus Christ, who is the faithful witness, the firstborn from the dead, and the ruler of the kings of the earth. To him who loves us and has freed us from our sins by his blood.

Revelation 1:4–5 NIV

As I lay on my face before Him, it was as if Jesus could see through me, reading all the thoughts of my heart. My whole body was shaking. I felt so unworthy to be in His presence. He was revealing Himself to me—a woman. But I did not know whether I would be judged or whether He would say, "Well done, good and faithful servant." But He showed me His mercy, which surrounds His throne and triumphs over judgment. Knowing my thoughts, He spoke to my heart and reminded me of His character—that He is gracious and compassionate, slow to anger and rich in love. He radiated an amazing love that contained deep acceptance. I felt neither condemnation nor shame.

> "Do you want to go back or stay here in heaven?" Jesus asked.

At first I hardly dared to look at Jesus, but after a time I felt my body being lifted up. Then I was standing before Him. As He smiled at me, relief poured over my soul.

"Welcome home, Samaa," He said in a voice sweet and gentle, yet also powerful, like the sound of many waters. He opened His arms to me. His beautiful eyes were like blazing fires of consuming love that overwhelmed me. Like a magnet, His love drew me in, melting my heart and transforming me from the inside out. Embraced by Love, I started to weep.

"Do you want to go back or stay here in heaven?" Jesus asked.

Then He showed me my life. As if seeing snapshots of a movie, I watched myself growing up. The nineteen years I'd lived passed in front of my eyes. After seeing the choices I had made, I realized I had been living for my own agenda and repented.

Oh, Lord Jesus, I'm so sorry. Please forgive me. All my life I've been living for myself—my ways, my dreams, my desires, my plans. But it's not about me. It's all about You. As I died for You, I want to live for You. Please give me another chance to live for Your will alone, Jesus. I was shaking so much, no words could come out of my mouth. But I knew He heard my heart.

Then He showed me another scene—my whole family, some of whom weren't saved yet. Finally I saw myself, dead from the bomb blast, and then glimpsed my parents', siblings' and other relatives' reactions. It broke my heart to see their pain.

Oh no, they can't take it, I thought, and instantly Jesus revealed to me that they, too, would be in heaven one day, reminding me of His promise in Acts 16:31. He wanted me to go back for my family for their salvation, but also for the salvation of *His* family, which is multitudes! God is all about family, from Genesis to Revelation. As Revelation 5:9 (NIV) says:

> "You are worthy to take the scroll and to open its seals, because you were slain, and with your blood you purchased for God persons from every tribe and language and people and nation."

And Revelation 7:9 (NIV) says:

> After this I looked, and there before me was a great multitude that no one could count, from every nation, tribe, people and language, standing before the throne and before the Lamb. They were wearing white robes and were holding palm branches in their hands.

The multitude was His children who were lost on the earth. He wanted me to go back for the nations, which is His inheritance (see Psalm 2:8).

I understood nothing I had was mine. My life and future, my friends and family, heaven and earth, all belongs to the Lord. All the while I was in heaven no sound came from my mouth. I never spoke out loud. We communicated heart to heart. In heaven I experienced joy, peace and love overwhelming.

Everything in me wanted to stay forever. After all, His presence is my home. He is my everything—Alpha and Omega. But He is also a Gentleman. He never forced me but gave me the freedom to choose. As I told Him my choice—that I wanted to go back to earth and be a witness for Him—I was motivated by love, not a sense of duty. Jesus is the worthy Lamb who was slain to receive the reward for His suffering. I knew that I had been martyred for Jesus and that my reward would be great in heaven. Jesus is my great reward!

But I also wanted to live for Him. I thought He would say no, but I was wrong. It was God who put the desire in my heart to fulfill His calling. As it says in Psalm 37:4, "Delight yourself in the LORD; and He will give you the desires of your heart." He is my Desire!

Jesus is my great reward!

"All right, see you soon," He said.

Immediately a fresh wave of love washed over me. It felt so easy to talk to Him, to communicate, like a child speaking to her Father. So often, I realized, we make our relationship with Jesus complicated. But it is so simple. Like Jesus said in John 14:9, "Anyone who has seen me has seen the Father" (NIV).

All was eternally peaceful. I no longer experienced the dimension of time. The moment I was with Jesus, I existed in the eternal present.

Ecclesiastes 3:11 (NIV) says:

> He has made everything beautiful in its time. He has set eternity in the human heart; yet no one can fathom what God has done from beginning to end.

I don't know how long I was in heaven. It felt as if I was there for an eternity. God is, after all, outside of time: "With the Lord a day is like a thousand years, and a thousand years are like a day" (2 Peter 3:8 NIV).

I understood that Jesus Himself *is* Heaven, and that without Him it is not heaven. He is the center of everything.

When I was in His presence, it was all I wanted, and I wasn't aware of the rest of my surroundings. People have asked if I saw the New Jerusalem and twenty-four elders talked about in Revelation, or family members, angels, clouds of witnesses, flowers or golden streets. It was all there, but my eyes were fixed on Jesus, the King of kings and Lord of lords. It was as if Jesus was a brilliant diamond—or a jasper stone and sardius as described in Revelation 4:3. His beauty, dazzling and excellent and radiating holiness and splendor, totally captivated me. All of my affection and attention focused on Him. Everything else in heaven was like precious stones, their glory fading in beauty beside the beautiful diamond that reflected light from every angle. Jesus was ethereal, but at the same time real and tangible.

If Jesus asked me again, now, if I wanted to go back to earth or stay in heaven, I would never ask to come back. He is my Dearly Beloved, my Bridegroom, Lover of my soul, my life, my all in all, my Dream, my Vision, my Heaven! Being with Him in heaven, though, made me one with Him in a way I could never have imagined. I thought what He thought, I dreamed what He dreamed, I felt what He felt and I prayed what He prayed.

When I died for Him, it was so sudden, and then, in a flash, I was in heaven. Going back to live on earth would be much harder—to walk by faith, step by step, and to be obedient. I knew I was no longer of this world. From that point on I died to my own will and started living these Scriptures:

> I am torn between the two: I desire to depart and be with Christ, which is better by far; but it is more necessary for you that I remain in the body.
>
> Philippians 1:23–24 NIV

I have been crucified with Christ and I no longer live, but Christ lives in me. The life I now live in the body, I live by faith in the Son of God, who loved me and gave himself for me.

Galatians 2:20 NIV

What is more, I consider everything a loss because of the surpassing worth of knowing Christ Jesus my Lord, for whose sake I have lost all things. I consider them garbage, that I may gain Christ.

Philippians 3:8 NIV

I will wait on earth for the return of my beloved Bridegroom, who will come back for His bride. I can't wait for our wedding day to come and see His face again!

Oh, how I miss Jesus. . . .

18

FIGHTING FOR MY LIFE

At the exact time that the second bomb went off Adila had been outside helping the injured from the first bomb. She suddenly felt she needed to intercede for me, to fight for my life in prayer. She had no idea that I had experienced death but was simply being obedient to the still, small voice of the Holy Spirit. Adila was praying out loud as the Holy Spirit interceded through her. Prayers burst from within her and she only stopped when she felt at peace. Such prayer (see James 5:16; Romans 8:26–27) can even bring a dead person back to life.

That day, the same Spirit that resurrected Jesus, who is the resurrection and the life, raised me from death. And I declared the truth of these verses:

> Death has been swallowed up in victory. "Where, O death, is your victory? Where, O death, is your sting?" . . . Thanks be to God! He gives us the victory through our Lord Jesus Christ.
>
> 1 Corinthians 15:54–55, 57 NIV

I shall not die, but live, and declare the works of the LORD.

Psalm 118:17 NKJV

Jesus said to her, "I am the resurrection and the life; he who believes in Me will live even if he dies."

John 11:25

When my spirit came back into my body, I started to hear voices. "Wake up, Samaa, wake up!" they shouted, shaking me.

Suddenly I was no longer in that place of peace and glory. I returned to this world. My broken body was still where the bomb had thrown me. Slowly I began to feel terrible pain, and it took my breath away. I could hardly see or open my mouth.

Members from the church carried me outside. It seemed as if a film was slowly covering my eyes. I was going blind. My skin was burned, revealing my flesh like raw meat. Blood poured from wounds in my head, and my body was full of splinters and metal. I remember the strong smell of burning hair and skin. What was left of my hair was standing on end, a short frizzled mass, where once it had been long and silky, falling below my waist.

In the shock I stood and started walking, though now I don't know how I did it. I remember realizing I was naked and feeling my beautiful dress reduced to rags. Just as I was about to collapse, some people picked me up and started carrying me to the church minibus, which was taking the injured people to the hospital. It was the grace of God that we had the buses, as the ambulance was called but never came.

"Samaa!" Adila called in shock as she saw me.

I began to weep as I heard her voice.

"Cover me," I whimpered. The pain took the wind out of me. As I spoke, blood poured out of my mouth.

Adila carefully put her jacket over my body. She was so shaken at the sight of me that she tried hard to hold back tears. "Don't worry. Everything is going to be all right. God is in control. He is Sovereign," she said, in faith, despite what I looked like.

Her words comforted me, and I felt the presence of Jesus Emmanuel.

Jesus spoke to my heart, saying, "Samaa, I'm here with you. I will never leave you. I will be with you always, to the end. Don't be afraid."

My heart was filled with peace as I was taken into the church bus. Adila couldn't go with me as the bus was full of the wounded and dying. I was like the blind man in Mark 8:24 who said, "I see people; they look like trees walking around" (NIV). I was the same, my eyesight was fuzzy, but what I could make out horrified me. There were people with terrible injuries. One man had his right eye blown out. He was holding what was left of it to his face. Another woman whose leg was blown off below her knee was holding on to me and weeping. My other friend was in a coma, and her brother was crying over her. And my friend Iaub was burned badly. In agony he started praying in the Spirit while he was sitting next to me.

It felt as if I was living in a nightmare. Yet, despite my suffering, I started quietly singing a worship song: "Jesus is here right now, and His mighty power is here to heal me, restore me, deliver me and save me." The words croaked out of my mouth. I knew there was power in praising God. It was easy to praise Him when all was going well. However, when it's a sacrifice to praise Him, in the midst of trials and difficult circumstances, the breakthroughs in growing our faith come.

Worship is truly warfare in the spiritual realm, such as the apostle Paul experienced in prison:

> About midnight Paul and Silas were praying and singing hymns to God, and the other prisoners were listening to them. Suddenly there was such a violent earthquake that the foundations of the

prison were shaken. At once all the prison doors flew open, and everyone's chains came loose.

Acts 16:25–26 NIV

Just as Paul had been set free from chains in prison as he praised, so I was set free from the chains of pain as I sang. David, too, praised God whatever the circumstances, and God gave me the grace to do the same.

I had been closest to the bomb, but miraculously I could still hear. Many had gone deaf from the blast. (Later I was told there had been plenty of wax in my ears that had protected the eardrums. By cleaning my ears with cotton swabs, I had actually pushed back the wax further into my ears. Eventually doctors pulled all the wax from my ears, and I've never had a problem with wax before or after. I marveled knowing how God had protected my hearing.)

Iman had been near a window when the bomb went off. The force of the explosion knocked her to the ground, and some glass from the shattered windows gashed her forehead. Her face was covered in blood, and she was taken to the hospital as well.

I was sent to a hospital for my burns, but the staff wouldn't admit me. I was left alone and had no strength to move.

A doctor looked at the blood oozing out of my head and said to a nurse: "She is about to die. She needs surgery urgently."

My whole body was red with fresh blood. The jacket Adila had given me was soaked through. You couldn't see any skin on my body—only burned, blistering flesh. I was in intense pain. The burns on my body were so serious that I still felt as if my body was on fire. Quickly I was transferred in the church vehicle to the General Hospital so they could deal with my head wound.

Once we got to the hospital I was carried inside. Thankfully Iman eventually found me at the second hospital and tried to comfort me. The doctors were not doing anything, so she cried out, begging someone to help me. She knew I wouldn't survive if I lost any more blood, so she went off in search of attention for me.

Ironically, only two days before, I had been in the hospital giving blood. One of the deacons was very ill and needed blood, so many of us at the church volunteered. As I had the same blood type as our deacon, they needed to take more, and it felt like they almost drained me dry. I had been very weak afterward and was still not feeling completely myself on the day of the explosion.

"Help me, please," I cried to the nurses I could hear passing by, but none would listen.

As it was Sunday, there weren't many doctors around. I began to feel cold and started to shake. I had been fasting that day and was suddenly very thirsty.

"Please, can I have some water?" I asked anyone who would listen. My mouth was dry and full of blood. Even talking was painful.

No one helped me. I realized that the medical staff presumed I was so close to death I would not survive. They were inundated with injured people from the bomb blast and clearly must have felt that it would be a waste of time trying to save me.

Lord, help me, I cried inwardly.

All of a sudden everything went black as I passed out, slumping to the floor.

19

Healing Miracles

I woke up on the operating table. By now my eyesight was completely gone. I was terrified, sitting in darkness, only able to hear voices. Groaning, I became aware once more and was stricken by intense pain.

After I had collapsed, my sister Iman had been successful in getting the medical staff to help me. They agreed to clean up my wounds and stitch me up as best they could. I had been given an anesthetic but it was wearing off, and I could feel the doctor trying to remove the sand, glass and bomb shrapnel from my head wounds. He was shaking as he worked on me. The sight of my open head was horrific.

The smell of burned hair and flesh permeated the room. I could hear the doctor and nurses but couldn't see them because I was now completely blind. "What a shame. She must have been a beautiful girl, and now she's ruined," said one of the doctors.

I knew I was naked and felt so embarrassed. All of my dignity was gone.

The News

Neighbors heard about the bomb on the radio. They knew my sisters and I had been going to the church, so they ran to tell my family. Muqaddas was home on her own. Papa was out, and my mother was at our grandmother's, an hour and a half away in another city.

Muqaddas ran down the corridor to another apartment in our building where Malika was visiting a friend. "Malika, there was a bomb at the church! People died," she announced. "I don't know if our sisters are okay," she cried.

Malika immediately left the apartment and ran outside to catch a bus to the church, all the time praying for our safety. She got off at a stop nearby, and as she was getting nearer, saw a neighbor of ours running from the direction of the church.

"What happened?" she asked, noticing the blood on his clothes.

"There were two bombs that exploded. It's terrible—so many dead," he said, wiping tears from his eyes.

"Do you know about my sisters?" she asked, hoping he would give her some good news.

"Sorry, I just don't know! So many have been injured and died."

By this time Malika felt sick with terror. She didn't know what she would find when she got there. When she arrived, the police had already cordoned off the entrance to the building. She saw more people with blood on their clothes, women and children crying and police making sure no one left the area or went inside the building as it was still dangerous.

"Stop! If you go any further, I will shoot!" a policeman ordered as Malika tried to get close to the bombed building. In desperation she told him her sisters were inside, but he was adamant she could not enter and told her she must leave immediately.

Just as Malika was about to give up, some church members called to her.

"Do you know where my sisters are?" she asked desperately.

"Samaa and Iman are in the hospital. I think Adila is there, too," one of them said.

"Dear Lord, help them," Malika prayed, her worst fears realized. She made her way straight to the hospital and found Iman, who told her I was in the ICU. When she tried to see me, the nurses refused to let her enter, but Malika somehow sneaked through and made it to my bedside.

> "Dear Lord, help them," Malika prayed.

"Oh, Lord!" She wept as she saw me. I was unrecognizable—my face blackened and swollen, covered in fresh blood. Malika immediately started praying, but before long a nurse caught her and made her leave. She decided not to tell my mother, because my appearance might be too shocking for her to take.

However, Mubarak felt Mama should know, and when Mama returned from our grandmother's, she was told the truth. My mother fainted in shock. As she came around, she insisted on being taken to the hospital straightaway but never could have prepared herself for what she was about to see.

My battered, swollen and bloody body was horrifying. At first my parents didn't believe it was me. When they realized it was their daughter, Mama's heart gave way, and she collapsed on the ground in shock. Quickly a doctor picked her up, and she was rushed to another ward to be cared for. Her father had died young, of a heart attack, and she had a weak heart, too.

My father clutched his chest, feeling that he, too, might have a heart attack. Thankfully he didn't, but he still needed treatment for the shock. My brother Musa's wife, who was heavily pregnant at the time, was so traumatized when she saw me that she nearly lost their baby.

While being treated, my parents were taunted by the Muslim medical staff, who said what was happening was their own fault because their children were infidels. Many of the nurses and doctors believed that we had been paid to go to church and had turned away from Islam because we were offered money. They would have been shocked to know the truth—that we were in fact *giving* our tithes and offerings to the church as an act of worship to Jesus.

Some foreign Christian doctors came to the hospital when we were first admitted, offering to treat us for free. The hospital refused, even though they did not have sufficiently trained doctors to meet our needs. We did not have a national health service and had to pay for all treatment, so when all the bomb victims came in, that meant a lot of money for the hospital.

The doctors had told Malika that I would not live because my injuries were too serious. "If your sister does not respond today, we don't think there is a chance for her," one of the nurses said.

They had done all they could, and told my family to prepare for my funeral.

That evening my friends prayed through the night for my life. As the news of the bomb reached the outside world, others began to pray for our church.

During my first few days in the hospital, I was in intensive care, and my family could not stay with me. They waited in the corridor outside my room, numb with fear. The hours seemed endless for my parents as they watched the clock, praying and willing me to show signs of life.

But the next morning there was a breakthrough. A nurse and doctor were checking my condition when suddenly I spoke. "I'm hungry," I said in a hardly audible whisper.

They looked at each other with mouths wide open, wondering if they had imagined what I just said. "What would you like to eat?" the doctor asked.

"Kebab . . . strawberries and chocolate," I replied weakly.

The Bible shows that when people are raised from the dead, they are always hungry. When Jesus was resurrected and first appeared to the disciples, He asked for food. Also, in Mark 5:43 and Luke 8:55, Jesus told the family of the twelve-year-old girl He raised from the dead (Jairus's daughter) to bring her food right away. I was like Jesus and that girl.

> **The Bible shows that when people are raised from the dead, they are always hungry.**

The doctor said he would see what he could do and then went to tell my family the good news: Their daughter had turned a corner. I heard the joyful commotion outside my room and recognized the comforting voices of my family.

I was in and out of consciousness for three days. When my family first came to see me, they brought kebab, chocolate and strawberries, one of my favorite fruits. I couldn't eat any of it, though, as I was being fed intravenously.

Spiritually I was free, but physically the pain was excruciating. Added to this, I was blind, so I became very distressed when people visited me. I didn't know who they were. I remember hearing the rustle of someone sitting by my bed. "Who are you?" I asked, panic rising.

"It's your papa, my sweet one. Everything is going to be all right," said my father, taking my bandaged hand to comfort me.

I felt God's love through my father. He was with me night and day, making sure I was okay, holding my hand and kissing my forehead. It was almost as if he was asking my forgiveness for his persecution over the years. I held no bitterness toward him for how he had treated me. I knew God was melting his heart. We had been very close before I became a Christian. He had been so affectionate with me as a little girl—carrying me around piggyback—but my decision to follow Christ had brought a distance between us.

After the bomb our relationship was restored. He was the only one who was allowed to be with me in the ICU.

Hospital Treatment

The doctors had wrapped my burned, swollen body in bandages, covering blistered flesh. They and the nurses were Muslim. They knew why the other victims and I were in the hospital and that we had converted from Islam to Christianity. As a result they treated us very badly. When changing my dressings, a nurse with cold black eyes got scissors and roughly cut the bandages

> He was with me night and day, making sure I was okay, holding my hand and kissing my forehead.

before ripping them off my body, taking my flesh with them. I cried out in pain, but it didn't make any difference.

My strength came in remembering 1 Peter 1:6–7 (NIV):

In all this you greatly rejoice, though now for a little while you may have had to suffer grief in all kinds of trials. These have come so that the proven genuineness of your faith—of greater worth than gold, which perishes even though refined by fire—may result in praise, glory and honor when Jesus Christ is revealed.

"Curse on you, you traitor. This is a judgment from Allah. You deserve this," the nurses muttered.

Jesus said to pray for those who persecute you. And I prayed for them. I felt as if I was being tortured for my faith all over again. They continued, more roughly than before.

"Why are you doing this?" I screamed in pain. I didn't think I could take any more.

"Shut up, if you know what is good for you," was their reply.

Despite the pain they inflicted, my heart broke for them and the others who tortured me. I longed to share the love of Christ. "Even though you are ripping off my flesh, I will still tell you that Jesus loves you," I managed to say, gasping. "And I forgive you. You don't know what you are doing." I did not stop sharing the Gospel, even with those who were persecuting me. I was sustained through Romans 5:3–5 (NIV):

> Not only so, but we also glory in our sufferings, because we know that suffering produces perseverance; perseverance, character; and character, hope. And hope does not put us to shame, because God's love has been poured out into our hearts through the Holy Spirit, who has been given to us.

I had been to heaven! I had seen Jesus face to face! I could not hold back God's love and forgiveness.

I could not hold back God's love and forgiveness.

The doctors did not give me much care. At first they would not do any operation on my head unless my family paid a lot of money. However, the president of my country sent authorities to check on the bomb victims. After that, our treatment got better. Eventually those hurt by the bomb were given financial compensation by the government. It wasn't a lot, just enough to pay for my treatment and medication after I left the hospital, but it was a real blessing.

In the hospital we were kept under guard as the police feared the terrorists might try to come and finish us off.

Ten of my friends who had been near the bombs when they went off died instantly. Wafa, who had been standing next to me in the explosion, had his head blown off. He was found decapitated, clutching his Bible to his chest. "Precious in the sight of the LORD is the death of His godly ones" (Psalm 116:15). Nearly two hundred people were injured; fifty of those had life-threatening injuries like me. No one understood why I survived, as I had been closest to the bomb.

I was in and out of a coma. Each time I came around I would cry out to God for my healing, especially my eyesight. I couldn't bear the thought of being in the world and not being able to see. I believed I would see and held on to Isaiah 53:5: "By his wounds I am healed" (NIV).

My skin was burned, but I prayed for supernatural healing—for new skin to grow without any skin graft. As Mark 16:18 says, "They will lay hands on the sick, and they will recover," so I laid hands on myself and prayed for my own recovery.

My head hurt so badly that it felt as if it would explode, so I pleaded the blood of Jesus over my headache. I asked Him to wash all the pain away.

Ministers came and prayed as well, anointing me with oil (see James 5:14). We also had communion (see 1 Corinthians 11:23–26).

Whenever I was lucid, I cried out to God to heal my eyes. After three days, I began to see a faint light through my eyelids.

"Lord, thank You for opening my eyes!" I cried over and over again.

Slowly, as I praised Him, my eyes began to open. The doctors were amazed. They thought I would be blind for life. They had told my family that my eyes had been burned by the bomb and my blindness would be impossible to cure. I now have perfect eyesight! I truly wondered if I had been temporarily blind because, like the apostle Paul, I saw Jesus face to face. His face was as bright as the sun. I had read that Paul was also blind for three days after seeing Jesus:

> Saul got up from the ground, but when he opened his eyes he could see nothing. So they led him by the hand into Damascus. For three days he was blind, and did not eat or drink anything.
>
> Acts 9:7–9 NIV

My church family, my parents, brothers and sisters were with me constantly after my first six days in the ICU. They stayed the night, and when I started to be able to eat, brought me all my meals. Friends stood around my bed holding hands and praying out loud for me every day. They took shifts fasting and praying for the healing of everyone affected by the bomb.

My Muslim family members met friends from the church every day and were touched by the love and care they saw. One positive outcome from the bombing was that my father and older brothers were so saddened by nearly losing me that they gave up persecuting me from then onward.

"Samaa died for Jesus, so she will live for Him," said Papa, and my brothers agreed.

They witnessed my commitment to my new faith and began to grasp how important my relationship with Jesus was.

After those first critical few days, and the miraculous return of my sight, I did not continue to improve in the hospital. My head was like a drum, pulsating excruciating pain throughout my body. With no pain relief, I lay in agony on the bed, silent tears falling down my cheeks. I had been given many blood transfusions and later wondered whether it was my own blood from a few days earlier.

The Breaking Point

About a week after the bomb I felt I couldn't take any more pain. My whole body was swollen and blistered. I was still unrecognizable. Every time I lifted my head, I would vomit. The pain was so great I wasn't able to sleep. I was at the breaking point.

God knew and sent help.

I was told that someone who worked with the president was going to be visiting the hospital. I loved our president and prayed for him, but at that point I didn't want to see any visitors. All I wanted was to escape the pain.

However, instead of a government official, the "authority" was my dear American friend Dr. Kim. When he entered my room, it was like seeing an angel. My mouth formed the word *Papa*, but no sound came out. I was in so much pain, I couldn't even speak. All I could do was look into his eyes, my tears speaking a thousand words. I wept as I knew he would look after me. He, too, was crying—but trying to hold his tears—so moved by my condition.

When he entered my room, it was like seeing an angel.

When Dr. Kim heard about the bomb, he flew straight to my country from America. At first the hospital refused to let him touch or treat me, but as he stood by my bed, Dr. Kim quickly and gently inspected my head wound and saw that fresh blood was still seeping out. The doctors had made a half-hearted attempt to operate but had still left much of the bomb debris (such as small bits of glass, sand and dirt) in my head. Instead of finishing the job, they had just bandaged it up and left me.

Dr. Kim realized that I was on the point of death and that if he did not intervene, I would die.

Dr. Kim devised a plan and used his connections in government to get me out of the ward so he could operate on me. During the weekend, when the hospital had fewer staff on duty, with the help of friends and family, I and other injured friends were "smuggled" out of our wards.

We were taken by van to the new building to which we had been planning to move before the bombing. It was still under construction.

Every movement caused agony. Church members were careful carrying my stretcher, making sure I wasn't in any undue pain.

In a makeshift operating theater, with no electricity, Dr. Kim prepared to repair my wounds. I had been taught hairdressing by a professional hairdresser who was a Christian friend. While I was in the hospital, he came to shave some of my hair off. Before the operation, Dr. Kim gently shaved off the rest with a razor and washed my body with alcohol. The local doctors had been too nervous of my wound to shave my head. As soon as my singed hair was gone, I felt more peaceful. The smell of smoke in it was so disturbing. It took me right back to the explosion and made me feel sick to my stomach.

Dr. Kim cleaned the area around my head wound. He was so gentle and tender, like a father looking after his daughter. He was being helped by Rasul, a doctor and preacher with whom I had gone on medical missions. Rasul had been sitting right next to the first bomb but had gone to get his offering from the office in the floor below when the bomb exploded. If he had not forgotten his offering that day, he would have died. He had been outside when the second bomb detonated, and glass from a window fell on him, embedding itself in his back, but after it was removed and he was bandaged up, he recovered quickly.

Despite his injuries, he was still arrested and imprisoned like my sister Adila, but also released without charge.

Dr. Kim did one operation on my head, and then I was smuggled back into the hospital. The doctors turned a blind eye because they knew Dr. Kim had favor with the government. They feared getting in trouble with the authorities if they tried to stop him.

By the next weekend my sutures had burst, and I needed follow-up treatment. Again, I was smuggled out of the hospital. This time Adila was asked to help assist in the operation, as she had helped many times before during medical missions.

Even though I was her sister and it would be very hard to watch, she willingly said yes and held a flashlight in each hand over my head for three hours while Dr. Kim worked. It was exhausting, and her arms quickly grew tired, but she did not rest until the operation had finished. Adila prayed for me unceasingly as she watched my friend, Dr. Kim, try to coax the skin on my head closer and closer together in order to stitch it and cover the hole. The second operation took place in the building where the bomb had exploded. A surgical area had been set up on the first floor, but I felt very tense being back in the place of such trauma. I was under a local and not a general anesthetic, so I could talk and see what was happening around me.

Despite finding it emotionally difficult being back in the building, I was looked after with such compassion. It was such a different treatment from the nurses who were still persecuting me back at the hospital. I felt the love and timely mercy of God through Dr. Kim. He had come just when I needed him.

Miraculous Healing

After Dr. Kim treated me, the pain in my head started to subside. He had brought a special medicated cream from America for my burns, and each day someone from the church would put it on my skin, praying for me at the same time. I was getting better miraculously fast.

My fellow classmates from the university came to visit. At first they cried at seeing my ruined body. But after a while, when they witnessed my healing, they couldn't believe it and almost didn't recognize me.

One woman who was in the burn ward when I arrived noticed that my skin seemed to be recovering and that I didn't have scars or need skin grafts.

"How has your skin healed?" she asked me one day. She had many burns herself and had terrible scars over her body.

"It is Jesus—He is my Healer," I said and explained the Gospel to her.

"If He can heal, I would love Him to do that for me," she replied.

So I prayed for her healing and testified about the miracle-maker Jesus.

In the days that followed, the doctors were also amazed at what they were seeing in me.

> "The Great Physician healed me," I said, smiling. "Jesus is the same yesterday, today and forever."

"You have new skin; there are no scars!" one exclaimed when he examined me.

"The Great Physician healed me," I said, smiling. "Jesus is the same yesterday, today and forever" (see Hebrews 13:8).

God had given me new skin.

I stayed in the first hospital for about two weeks and then moved to another hospital for my burns. At both I was persecuted by the doctors and nurses. I rejoiced that the Lord was the source of my healing. The doctors could do the possible, and He would do the impossible.

Between friends and my family, one person would stay with me at all times. My sister Malika was a sensitive nurse, watching over me and reading to me when I couldn't sleep. I had been warned that the terrorists might come back and try to "finish us off," so at first I found it hard to sleep. I felt much better in the new hospital.

While there, I was marked with joy. I was drunk on God's Holy Spirit (see Romans 14:17). Joy and laughter are the currency of heaven, and they stayed with me when I came back to earth. The joy of the Lord was and is my strength and medicine. Often I would joke and laugh my loud contagious laugh in the middle of all the pain and discomfort.

"Why are you laughing?" people would ask, surprised.

"Would you prefer me to cry?" I'd ask, before bursting out in laughter again!

I would tell everyone about Jesus: the patients, doctors and nurses. Despite my pain I was on fire for God. I was transformed when I met Jesus. I now had an eternal perspective and mindset and didn't want anyone to not know Him. I had been to the most beautiful place imaginable with Jesus, and I wanted everyone on earth to experience it, too. My heart was in heaven, as it says in Colossians 3:1–4 (NIV):

> Since, then, you have been raised with Christ, set your hearts on things above, where Christ is, seated at the right hand of God. Set your minds on things above, not on earthly things. For you died, and your life is now hidden with Christ in God. When Christ, who is your life, appears, then you also will appear with him in glory.

My father gave one last try at asking my sisters and me to return to Islam.

After listening respectfully I replied, "If being a Muslim brought me salvation I would return, but Jesus is the only way to salvation. He is the way, the truth and the life, and I will follow Him."

> "If being a Muslim brought me salvation I would return, but Jesus is the only way to salvation."

My father shrugged, sighed and left the room. He knew then that we would never give in to his request. From that time onward he gave up fighting for us to return to Islam.

The police were doing their best to hunt the bombers, but were looking down all of the wrong avenues. They even came to the hospital to question those who had nearly died.

"Did you blow up the church?" asked a police agent as I lay in the hospital bed, face swollen and covered in bandages.

I couldn't believe what he was asking. "How could you think that?" I replied in shock.

Returning Home

After another month in the new hospital, I was able to go home. We had a neighbor who was a nurse and she would come over to give me my injections and change my bandages.

It took almost a year before I recovered fully both physically and emotionally from the bomb.

My new skin was very sensitive and tender for a while. For almost a year I could not go out into the sunlight, and even then I could go outside only if I wore total sunblock.

I was also very jumpy. Whenever I heard loud noises, even a balloon popping, my heart would race.

Once, a month after I was able to go out by myself, I was on a crowded bus. As we rounded a corner between home and a friend's house, a tire blew. The driver, looking for a place to pull out of traffic, continued to let the vehicle lumber awkwardly forward.

Jumping up from my seat with a scream, I couldn't understand why the others weren't running for the exit. Pushing and shoving, I elbowed my way to the door. Even though the bus had not stopped, I managed to yank the door open and jump to the curb.

Still not satisfied it was safe, I sprinted as fast as I could back around the corner we had just turned. Part of me knew this was irrational, yet I couldn't help myself. I'm sure the other passengers thought I was crazy, but at the time I thought something was wrong with them.

Stopping about a block away, I leaned against the wall. My heart pounded. My breath came in short gasps.

Mentally and spiritually I was not afraid, but my body's instinctive reaction to the sound of an explosion had betrayed me. I had peace in my heart, but for a time my body still reacted to any loud noise.

Another time I was sleeping at home when one of our gas heaters made a huge bang. I woke up instantly and, without thinking, ran as fast as I could, trying to get out of the apartment. My father caught me and tried to calm me down, saying it was just the heater, that I was safe. It took a while for him to convince me to go back to bed.

Apart from the irrational, emotional reminders, I did have one constant physical memorial of what I had been through and what a miracle my return to life represented: Although my skin was new, my hair never grew back over the scar on my head.

At first I would lay hands on the small, round, bald patch and pray for the hair to grow. But then I felt God say it was a mark of suffering and a remembrance of how He had healed and restored me.

He reminded me that Jesus still had the scars from His crucifixion on His side, His hands and His feet. God let me recognize that I carry the scar on my head from the explosion as a mark of love, to share in His suffering—and share when His glory is revealed.

God's Word sustained me during my recovery time, including 1 Peter 4:12–14 (NIV):

> Dear friends, do not be surprised at the fiery ordeal that has come on you to test you, as though something strange were happening to you. But rejoice inasmuch as you participate in the sufferings of Christ, so that you may be overjoyed when his glory is revealed. If you are insulted because of the name of Christ, you are blessed, for the Spirit of glory and of God rests on you.

I felt the Lord had said I would be completely healed, and I believed His words. He had revealed Himself to me as Jehovah-Rapha, Healer (see Exodus 15:26). I was supposed to be unable to walk. I was supposed to be deaf and blind and burned.

I was supposed to be dead.

It was a miracle that I survived and that today my body is fully restored.

> **I felt the Lord had said I would be completely healed, and I believed His words. He had revealed Himself to me as Jehovah-Rapha, Healer.**

As I got stronger, I appreciated every day, no longer taking my time for granted. It was an enforced sabbatical—a time to rest, pray, worship and read my Bible. I was like King David, searching for God's heart, as recorded in Psalm 42: "As the deer pants for the water brooks, so my soul pants for You, O God."

I missed Jesus, even though He is with me always through the presence of the Holy Spirit. I wanted to be back with Him in paradise. I was homesick for heaven.

I sang Psalm 84:1–2 (NIV):

How lovely is your dwelling place,
LORD Almighty!
My soul yearns, even faints,
for the courts of the LORD; my heart and my flesh cry
    out
for the living God.

Before the bomb I had been constantly on the go with different ministries, mission trips, coaching, teaching, going to university, etc. I had been exhausted and never took a break. Now I knew I needed the sabbatical Hebrews 4:4 talks about—"On the seventh day God rested from all his works" (NIV)—and incorporated it into my lifestyle to take time to minister to the heart of God and return to the great commandment to love the Lord with all my heart, all my mind and all my soul.

20

DELIVERANCE

The first day I was in the hospital Adila spent in jail. After the bombing, the police arrested anyone who had remained. They were taken to a local police station, and Adila, along with church leaders, was charged as a suspect.

There was no comfort for her. Along with the terror she had just experienced, she was now persecuted for being a Christian. The policeman told her the bomb was what she could expect because she had left Islam. Despite the way they were treated, Adila and the other members still used the opportunity to preach to the policemen.

When Adila first arrived in the prison, she thought one of the special agents was our uncle, who also worked for the government. She was mistaken, but at the time she was sure it was him.

"Uncle, Uncle! It's me, Adila," she cried when she saw him.

The man laughed at her. "Why are you calling me 'uncle'? I am not your uncle." He ridiculed her.

"Don't you recognize me, Uncle?" she asked again.

The other policemen watched what was happening and assumed he was really her uncle. The man became angry but also embarrassed and told her again she must be mistaken.

Adila was with a friend named Nasiba, meaning "Noble." Nasiba tried to share the Gospel with the police, but they mocked and threatened her.

"We just need to sleep with you, and then we will become one and we will be Christians, too, won't we?" laughed one of the main guards, pulling off his belt, about to rape her.

As he went to grab Nasiba, violent indignation replaced fear in my sister. "What are you doing?" Adila demanded fiercely. "You are supposed to be protecting us!" She shielded Nasiba from the men.

"Who are you to speak to him like that?" shouted another guard. "You need to respect authority!"

Before Adila had time to duck, he slapped her hard on the face, knocking her to the concrete floor.

"You did it, didn't you? You planted the bomb. Confess!" He punched the breath out of her.

From her position on the floor, Adila looked up at the man, straight into his eyes, and said with authority from the Holy Spirit: "Jesus *loves* you."

As she spoke these words, the room became quiet. It was as if the fear of the Lord came over the guard, and he suddenly lost his nerve. He quickly turned away, not able to look her directly in the eyes.

"Jesus *loves* you."

"Bring her to the basement!" he commanded.

207

Adila's heart sank as she knew that was where people were raped and even killed.

"Why were you in a church?" he asked when they were in the basement.

Adila boldly told him her testimony, telling him about Jesus and His love.

"What you are telling me is treason," he said coldly. "I could kill you for what you have said. I could rape you. I could do anything. Aren't you afraid?"

Adila knew God was with her and with a supernatural boldness replied, "I'm not afraid."

Her words did not stop him. In anger he grabbed her by the throat before throwing her to the ground and kicking her. "Ready to tell the truth now?" he jeered.

Adila winced and groaned as she was hit, but still she prayed for him, that he might know Jesus. After enduring interrogation and beating, she was taken to a cell where others from church also were held. At first all the believers were together, and they hugged and prayed and then tried to get some sleep on the stiff wooden benches.

Then the police decided to separate everyone, and Adila was moved to a dark cell alone.

The next morning, after 24 hours in jail, Adila was released and came straight to see me in the hospital. She sneaked into my room and that night slept on the floor by my bed in the ICU. Bloodied and bruised herself, she prayed for me through the night.

A Miraculous Release

The next day police came to the hospital room and arrested her again.

Our coach was in jail for three days after the explosion and was persecuted for his faith in being a missionary. Adila spent three nights in jail before eventually being let out without charge on the morning of the fourth day. It was a miracle how she was released: Adila felt the Lord tell her to leave.

"Okay," she said but didn't know how she could. In faith she pushed open the door of the cell where they had been kept. Usually it was guarded by policemen, but no one was there.

She kept walking and bumped into two policemen she knew. Adila started talking to them like friends as she walked by, not as if she had been arrested. Amazingly they did not see anything unusual about her, so she kept on walking. She knew there was still a big iron gate with security guards that she would have to get through to get out.

But as she got to the main door of the prison, there was not one policeman there. It was empty. Calmly Adila tried the huge door, and it opened. She ran out into the fresh air of the city.

Later she told me that her miraculous escape from jail reminded her of the apostle Peter's escape in Acts 12:6–17.

Adila was able to assist Dr. Kim with his other operations as well. It turned out that he had treated the "Uncle" police agent in the past and when "Uncle" heard our friend was in the city, he contacted him to ask for treatment. Dr. Kim agreed.

When the police agent came for treatment, he was startled to see Adila. "You see, your 'uncle' has come back," the agent said to my sister, smiling sheepishly.

Adila was amazed at the favor God had given her with this man and continued to tell him about Jesus, her Savior.

Bombing Details

I was still recovering when the bombers were found after they blew up a vehicle and planted bombs in other churches in the city. The young men were caught and identified by members

209

of our church. They had been studying at the main mosque in the city.

All were sentenced to death.

It was difficult for us to think they had been the enemy among us, coming to our services for the month before the bombing. They had only been pretending to be interested in Jesus while they were studying the building to see where they could plant the bombs.

Adila filled in some of the details for me.

"The bombers placed three of the bombs the day before the explosions, when most people were resting after the Friday night of prayer. The bomb that went off first was left under a pew in a backpack during the morning service.

"The Saturday afternoon when the bombs were being placed was exactly the time I was feeling so ill. I'd had a nightmare and seen a white man wearing dark clothing. He was warning me that something very terrible was about to happen. I woke up suddenly from the dream and lay trembling in my bed. It was very real, and the sense of danger so intense that I was physically shaking."

Tears filled Adila's eyes as she told me the rest of the story. "When I looked at the clock, I realized Saturday choir practice had already started, so I quickly got my things together and ran to the rehearsal. I saw you there but didn't want to worry you. I was just happy to be surrounded with people and hoped I would soon shake off the feeling of unease, but I was still trembling by the time I got to the rehearsal room."

On Saturday night Adila, so sensitive to the Holy Spirit's leading, barely slept and woke up early with the same feeling of imminent evil she'd felt after the nightmare the day before. She got up to go to the 5:00 a.m. prayer meeting in the sanctuary and was the first to arrive. She prayed in tongues until she felt lighter in her spirit but had to return to bed as she had begun to feel weak with fever.

Iman filled in the rest of the details for me. On the day of the bombing, she had been at the door welcoming people. She had seen one of the terrorists with the backpack that morning but thought nothing of it at the time.

Forgiving the Bombers

The terrorists wanted to destroy our building because they thought that would destroy us and our faith. But as Isaiah 54:17 says, "No weapon that is formed against you will prosper; and every tongue that accuses you in judgment you will condemn. This is the heritage of the servants of the LORD."

The terrorists' plan was to plant bombs in all the churches in the city, and ours had been the first.

In spite of the many deaths and injuries from their bombs, we showed mercy to them and wrote a letter to our president, asking for their lives to be spared as they were sentenced to death for their crime.

The end result is that they were not killed. However, they are in prison for life. I am praying that they will encounter Jesus, the God of love, and be set free from their captivity to darkness and brought to the light of God's truth.

I had already forgiven the bombers. As Jesus prayed at the cross, "Father, forgive them; for they do not know what they are doing" (Luke 23:34). Since I myself had experienced God's forgiveness, how could I not choose to forgive my enemies? I've learned that forgiveness is a choice, not a feeling. It brings with it freedom from the prison of bitterness. The God of love I serve died for those terrorists as well as for me. I, too, was once God's enemy, but He made me His friend when I was reconciled to Him through the death of His Son (see Romans 5:10–11). By His grace, I followed His example and released forgiveness to those who had planned to kill us.

I never met the four terrorists. Because I was in recovery, I didn't have the opportunity to see them eye to eye. But Adila did.

However, God impressed upon me to pray Jesus' commandment from Matthew 5:43–44: "You have heard that it was said, 'Love your neighbor and hate your enemy.' But I tell you, love your enemies and pray for those who persecute you" (NIV).

> **By His grace, I followed His example and released forgiveness to those who had planned to kill us.**

After years of praying for terrorists to encounter the God of love, like Saul did when his name was changed to Paul, my prayers were answered. I met the ex-jihadist who worked with Al Qaeda and Osama bin Laden, who trained many terrorists. I knew he may even have trained the ones who bombed my church.

He shared his story with me. After killing so many Jews and Christians, he was prayed over by Christians. Then he was touched by the fire of God and had an encounter with the Lord. Jesus came to him in a dream, lit with beautiful light and joy, revealing that He is the way, the truth and the life. The Al-Qaeda-Jihadist repented and became a follower of Christ!

After hearing his story, I felt led by God to reconcile with him. "I forgive you, brother," I said, gazing into his eyes.

He fell on his knees and started weeping. "I am not worthy. I've killed so many in my life."

"As the Lord has forgiven you and I forgave you, too," I said, "now you must extend the forgiveness you have received to yourself."

Then I shared how I, too, was not worthy of God's mercy, yet He had mercy on me. I prayed with him, "Forgive us our sins, for we also forgive everyone who is indebted to us" (Luke 11:4 NKJV).

How grateful I am that the Lord is good, kind, loving and forgiving.

21

MIRACULOUS TRANSFORMATIONS

Our church later moved to a different piece of land. We met in a new building and installed a scanner, just as in an airport, so we could identify if anyone was carrying a weapon. Gone were the days the building could be open 24/7, but God still showed His grace. The policemen assigned to protect us sat through each Sunday service and, as a result, most became Christians.

One day Jawid, meaning "Eternal," my teenage cousin, came to our house for a visit. His mother had died when he was about three, and his father, my uncle, had moved to Europe to try to make some money to support his five sons. He left his children in the care of my grandmother.

My cousin had recently been diagnosed with epilepsy and had frequent fits—sometimes when he was alone in the streets of the city. On those occasions he had to be brought home by whoever found him.

Grandma was old and didn't have the strength to care for him and his brothers, so different members of the family had taken in the other boys. Adoption outside of families is not a concept in the Muslim culture. If a child's parents die, the immediate family is expected to take in the children as their own.

I loved my cousin and hated to see him suffering this way. My family had tried taking him to different doctors, even to the Imams and Mullahs, but no one could help. On the day Jawid arrived at our house we were all sitting together on the floor talking and eating when suddenly he jerked backward and started having a seizure. His whole body shook. His mouth fell open, and saliva flowed out. His eyes rolled back in his head.

Our family was amazed! They knew they had just seen a miracle.

Adila was with me. We looked at each other, both knowing what the other was thinking: Jawid's problem was spiritual, not physical. His fit was demonic. While Jesus was on this earth, "He went about doing good and healing all who were oppressed by the devil" (Acts 10:38).

We also believed the words of Mark 16:17–18:

> "These signs will accompany those who have believed: in My name they will cast out demons, they will speak with new tongues. . . . They will lay hands on the sick, and they will recover."

Even though the rest of our family was there in the room with us, Adila and I laid hands on our cousin and took authority over the demon, casting it out in Jesus' name.

Jawid shook furiously and then, after a little while, let out a long breath and lay peacefully on the ground. He was delivered completely and gave his life to Jesus.

Our family was amazed! They knew they had just seen a miracle. My mother was particularly touched, and from then on, when people came to our house, if they were sick, she would ask us to lay hands on them and pray for their healing.

A Breakthrough

I went with her one time to visit my grandmother in another city. She was suffering from high blood pressure and had such pains in her feet she couldn't stand for long.

Often my grandmother would tell my sisters and me that we had to marry a Muslim man and that we needed to return to Islam. This time when my mother told her, "Jesus heals. Let your granddaughter pray for you," my grandmother was quiet. She had never let me pray for her before, but I took her silence for acceptance, and prayed for her in the name of Jesus.

This was a huge change and a breakthrough. She got better, and although she did not become a believer at that time, her heart softened toward us.

The Accident

One spring evening a couple years after the bombing, my sisters and I had just returned from a worship time. We were eating a meal and getting ready for bed when I heard a knock at the door. I went to open it and saw a man I didn't know.

"Your father has been in an accident," he said. "It is very bad. You need to go to the hospital."

"But I don't know you," I queried. "How do you know my father?"

"I recognized him from the mosque," the man returned. "I recently moved into the area. Please, you have to come quick."

I knew Papa was having a meal with my brother Suleyman and his family, so I assumed this man had made a mistake. The

215

rest of the family was home, so Mama asked Malika and me to find out if the report was true. I quickly changed my clothes and, with Malika, went with the man in his taxi to the hospital.

When we arrived, my father was not there. I heard from the taxi driver what had happened. Father had been walking near the market in our city when he stepped out into the road to cross to the other side. Cars don't merely drive in my country; they race. One traveling at high speed smashed into him, hitting him in the stomach. My father flew into the air and landed head-first on the ground.

> **"Samaa, please pray for me. In Jesus' name."**

Everyone thought he was dead, and the man who had struck him drove off. No one wanted to take responsibility for my father as they feared being blamed for the accident if they took him to the hospital. Ambulances were still not running at that time as a consequence of the war, so my father was left bleeding and unconscious on the road for a long while. Finally a believer from church recognized my father and took him to the hospital in his own vehicle.

He was 68 and not as strong as he used to be. If no one had had mercy on him, he would have died. While Papa was taken to the hospital, the man who knew my father and witnessed the accident came to our house to tell us the news.

We found out later that Papa had been driven to a smaller hospital first. When they saw his injuries, they insisted he go to the main hospital in our city, where we were already waiting. It was important for a family member to be at the hospital as the doctors would not give any treatment without payment.

I prayed in tongues continually as we waited. After what seemed like eternity, a car pulled up, and my dad was carried out of the vehicle. He was covered in blood.

"Papa!" I choked. His condition was terrible.

He started to cry. "Samaa, please pray for me. In Jesus' name," he said, looking intently into my eyes.

We both knew the gravity of what he was saying.

I was shocked at his words. It was very humbling for him, and the first time he had acknowledged Jesus.

Papa had lost so much blood that he went into the ICU immediately. I was handed all his clothes and belongings. As they wheeled him away, the doctor told me to say a last good-bye to my father. They did not think he would survive.

I borrowed someone's phone to call my family, and they came straightaway. I was so relieved when my brothers arrived and took charge of the situation, as the hospital staff was asking for a lot of money for the surgery.

> **My father was alive. "Hallelujah!" I breathed when I heard.**

I knew I had to get away from the hospital and pray. I headed to the prayer room at church and prayed through the night, crying out to God for Papa's healing. I asked Him to have mercy on my father and spare his life.

In the morning, after having no sleep, I went back to the hospital. My father was alive. "Hallelujah!" I breathed when I heard.

However, the doctor said he would be paralyzed for the rest of his life as he had broken his back and legs, as well as his hand. He still had a concussion. I had hope, simply because he was alive when he should have died. My sisters and I prayed and fasted for him around the clock, and he began to get better. Our church also prayed and fasted.

The doctors could not disguise their surprise when Papa was transferred from the ICU to a general ward. After about a month in the hospital, Papa came home on a stretcher for home care. Although weak, he was not paralyzed.

This was a true miracle. All the doctors were amazed, as were the other patients, on seeing how fast my father was getting better. Many asked us to pray for them.

After the accident Papa did not work again. He also stopped practicing Islam. He no longer went to the mosque. He no longer fasted in Ramadan and gave up praying five times a day toward Mecca.

The doctor said he would be paralyzed for the rest of his life as he had broken his back and legs.

Instead, he came to the medical mission. Dr. Kim treated him, and church members shared the Good News with him.

After seventeen years of prayer, when I asked him if he wanted to invite Jesus into his heart as his Lord and Savior, he agreed. I couldn't believe what I was hearing. At first I thought he was joking, since he has a good sense of humor.

But when I asked him again, he answered seriously.

Through God's grace, I was able to lead him to the Lord. My father prayed with me, confessing Jesus as the Son of God. Now he says Jesus is his best friend, and he communes with Him daily. Hallelujah!

Papa became a different person. In the past, people had been very afraid of him because of his anger. But the Lord set him free from his temper. Instead, he became full of love and joy and much more gentle.

It has indeed been a miraculous transformation.

PROVISION BY HEAVENLY PROVIDER

During my recovery, friends would sometimes pick me up so I could go to church, and they would often visit me at home. Eventually I was well enough to get a job. I took a variety of different positions, from working in a shop selling clothes to being a hairdresser. Jesus Himself was a carpenter, and I'm sure He was an attentive, successful worker in wood. I, too, wanted to excel at whatever I did to glorify my Father in heaven. "And you shall remember the LORD your God, for it is He who gives you power to get wealth" (Deuteronomy 8:18 NKJV).

Three years after my heavenly experience I fasted for seven days for the salvation of the rest of my family and my direction in life. During that time, I heard God speak to me about the job I was to do. I felt I should apply to work at a specific restaurant as a waitress. I had heard about the waitressing job through Janan, meaning "Heart," my Christian friend who worked at the restaurant. The restaurant was one of the best in our city and the first to serve Mexican food. The prerequisite for the job was that you spoke English, because many foreigners came to eat there.

I wanted to be servant-hearted just like Jesus, and I wanted to understand what it meant to be a servant. So I chose to be a server. I had read in the Bible that we are to be kind to strangers and foreigners, and I longed to put that into practice in my job. I went for an interview and was given a job.

That restaurant became my mission field, and my desire was to serve the customers as if I was serving Christ. It was wonderful to have Janan there, too. We would pray together before every shift, holding hands and asking Jesus for His presence to be with us and for the salvation of our co-workers and customers.

I wanted the people who came into the restaurant to feel like kings and queens when I served them. Almost all of the regulars I befriended and with whom I shared the Gospel later came to church with me. One customer who worked for a foreign embassy was a lapsed Catholic. I invited him to church, and he was touched by God. Later he said, "Now I know what your secret is—it's Jesus who shines through you."

> **"Now I know what your secret is—it's Jesus who shines through you."**

Customers who were not believers in Jesus were drawn to me because of my joy. Some said it was my "aura," but none could really put into words what it was they were attracted to. When I got to know them better, I told them with a big smile, "It's Jesus. It's His presence I carry inside me."

I would always try to build relationships with the customers first, and then, when they asked me why I was different, I would tell them about the God of love. People were drawn to the joy, love and peace of the Holy Spirit in me.

I had such favor at the restaurant that customers would ask to be served by me instead of the other waitresses. I often received large tips and was able to bring money back to my family. With the money I also had an idea to give flowers to Jesus. There was already a ministry of flowers, but it depended on members of the congregation to buy them. Each week I would buy flowers and place them on the altar before the service. Iman would then hand them out to new believers who had come to the service.

To get the flowers I had to wake up early on Sunday morning, after having ordered the bouquets the night before, and go to collect them. I bought the best flowers that I could, and it was expensive, but like Mary in John 12:3 it was my extravagant worship to the King and such a joy. I became friends with the florists, and they often gave me flowers for myself free of charge. Lilac and roses were my favorite. Sometimes, if I was just walking past the shop, they would run out and bless me with flowers. This was particularly touching, since the florists were Muslims, and I'd told them I was buying the flowers for Jesus. Yet they still showed me so much favor. When I had established a good relationship with them, I started to share the Gospel and invited them to church. They eventually came to the medical mission that was held in the church.

The restaurant prospered while I worked there. Despite the fact that I was enjoying it so much, Janan and I still suffered from persecution. The chef and most of the other co-workers in the kitchen were Muslims. They would call us the infidel, saying we were fools to become Christians. If they'd had the power, they would have fired us, but our boss was American and happy with us, so we were safe. In the end their hearts softened toward us, and they ended up calling me "Pastor Samaa." They came to me whenever they had problems.

During times of persecution, I found my strength in God.

Bible School

In the long term I had plans to go to Bible school. My dream was to study in America, because I wanted to go to a school

221

with a Christian foundation, and there were none like that in my country.

By this time I had started going to a new European church plant in my city. After the bomb our church had moved to our other property, but the government wanted to take our building. We were under strong persecution. My sisters had some friends who went to the European church—they did not have a building but met in a home. After the meeting, we felt we should move to that church and spoke to our pastor to get his blessing, which he gave us because he loved us.

The European missionaries started talking about a Bible school at the church in our city and said I should attend. I told them I wanted to go abroad for Bible school, but then I kept on bumping into the missionaries at the most unexpected places around town. Each time they would say, "Samaa! Bible school! You need to come!"

"Is this what You have for me?" I asked God.

I was seeing them so frequently that it caught my attention. "Is this what You have for me?" I asked God.

I had felt the Lord say not to put off for tomorrow what can be done today. He was asking me to lay down my place at university and trust Him with my future.

The next time I saw the missionaries they asked me one more time, "Samaa, when are you going to realize you need to be at Bible school?"

"Now!" I replied, laughing. "I am coming."

After a year working in a restaurant I enrolled at the Bible school in our city and changed from working full-time to part-time at the restaurant. Adila and I had paid for Iman and Muqaddas to go the year before. I was looking forward to what God had for me and knew it would be the best. I also sensed that studying the Bible would be an important foundation for my future, whatever that might be.

At the end of that year I knew it was time to lay down my job at the restaurant. When I prayed about it, I felt the Lord say I was coming into a new season. In the winter, I told my boss I was leaving. My co-workers and I all cried on my final day. Though God had blessed me so much at the restaurant, it was now time to move on.

23

Acts of Faith

Studying the Bible opened my eyes to many things. One of the most significant was that God began to increase my love for the Jews.

Historically the Jews are enemies of Muslims. I was brought up to hate them, but even as a little girl, I refused and loved them. We had Jewish neighbors, and they were my friends.

"Why must I hate them? What have they done to me?" I would ask to the annoyance of the Mullah.

It wasn't until I met Jesus that I understood His desire for restoration between the Jews and Muslims, which would be, in effect, the reconciliation between the lineage of Isaac and Ishmael. We who are Christians are all called into the ministry of reconciliation: "All this is from God, who reconciled us to himself through Christ and gave us the ministry of reconciliation" (2 Corinthians 5:18 NIV).

I saw that as He reveals Himself to the Muslims (those who follow the religion of most of the sons of Ishmael) through dreams and visions, they would provoke the Jews (sons of Isaac) to jealousy when they see former Muslims knowing God intimately. I believe that, through this divine intervention, there will be a worldwide revival in the last days.

> "In the last days, God says, I will pour out my Spirit on all people. Your sons and daughters will prophesy, your young men will see visions, your old men will dream dreams. Even on my servants, both men and women, I will pour out my Spirit in those days, and they will prophesy. . . . And everyone who calls on the name of the Lord will be saved."
>
> Acts 2:17–18, 21 NIV

I long to go to Israel someday, as the Gospel was birthed there and then taken to the ends of the earth. I now also believe that the Good News will be brought back from the ends of the earth to Israel, since God says clearly in Romans chapters 9–11 that He has a plan and a purpose for the Jews and the nation of Israel. I pray daily for their salvation. "Salvation is from the Jews" (John 4:22), and Jesus is a Jew!

An Unexpected Provision

I wanted Adila, Malika and another friend, Shakila, meaning "Beautiful," to come to Bible school with me, but they didn't have any money. Miraculously I was given a large sum of money from a friend who supported my dream to go to America and study there. I used that money to start from where I was at home, not despising the small beginnings. He was amazed when I told him how perfect the timing was. It was enough to pay for my sister's fees as well as my own and Shakila's.

God provided for me financially in the most unusual ways at Bible school—one of which was modeling. Adila and I had a friend, Zakiyya, meaning "Pure," who was an aspiring actress and model. Zakiyya, a classmate of Adila's, had recently become a Christian after we had invited her to church with us. She was persecuted by her parents for her new faith, but her two older brothers also became believers and started coming to tae kwon do with us. Zakiyya's mother would not let me or my sister in her house but would scream abuse at us from her door for turning her children into the infidel. Our friend and her brothers held firm. Even when they were beaten by men from the mosque, they did not stop evangelizing. We tried to support them as best we could.

In winter that year there was a huge casting for models taking place in our city. They were advertising on TV, radio and in the press, describing the requirements needed for the girls they were looking for.

"Please come with me," Zakiyya pleaded with Adila and me.

"Sure, we'll be there for you," I said, smiling.

On the day of the casting hundreds of beautiful girls lined up waiting to enter the tall building in the center of our city.

> **God provided for me financially in the most unusual ways.**

We were wearing thick boots, which we stamped on the snow-covered ground to keep warm. Zakiyya was very nervous; this could be the beginning of her dream coming true.

However, as we came nearer to the entrance, we saw that you could only enter if you had signed up for the casting.

"Looks like you have to go alone," I said to Zakiyya.

"Oh no, please come in," she begged, desperate for us to stay with her.

So, laughing, Adila and I put down our details for the casting. But we didn't take it seriously.

The first test was to walk up and down in front of the judges, so they could look at our posture and how we held ourselves.

After we had paraded in front of them, Adila and I were accepted as models. The people from the modeling agency got excited about me, saying my face was beautiful and international. Even though I was not very tall, they thought I would work well. Adila, being tall and beautiful, was immediately accepted.

Then it was Zakiyya's turn. She was so nervous and timid she did not do well, and the judges told her she hadn't made it, even though she was stunning. She was distraught, coming to us with tears in her eyes, her dream crushed.

I didn't know what to do. I felt so bad that we had been given a job and had only been there to support our friend. I knew I had to do something, so boldly I walked up to the head of the organization. "Please give our friend another chance. If she is not accepted, then my sister and I will not work with you. But if you take her on, we will stay."

They looked at me without expression but with a shrug said, "Okay, let's test her again."

I was jubilant as I ran back to Zakiyya to tell her the good news.

We started praying, and this time, with more confidence, she walked in front of the judges and

"What is Your plan for this?" I asked the Lord.

was accepted. The three of us were now runway fashion models. Adila and I found the whole situation very funny, but we also felt God was in it. After all, it had to have been His favor that enabled us to get the job.

"What is Your plan for this?" I asked the Lord. I knew He had us in the fashion industry for a reason.

He told me that He wanted us to influence a different sphere of society. He loved the fashion designers and other models and longed for them to know about Him.

As I did different jobs, I worked with one fashion designer in particular. I was able to build a friendship with him, and we became very close. One evening after we had finished work and were walking down the road, he opened his heart to me. He told me he had been abused as a child and was now living a homosexual lifestyle. In our shame culture you can be stoned for being a homosexual, so he was trying to hide it. But now he was desperate.

I had so much compassion for him as he shared his story.

"Jesus loves you," I said. "He doesn't judge you. You just need to receive His forgiveness, forgive yourself and sin no more." I was reminded of the story of the harlot brought by the pharisees to Jesus. He didn't judge her and instead forgave her, showing her the love of God.

I led him through a prayer of repentance. Not long after we prayed, the designer entered a competition to have a fashion show in Europe. The competition was on a Sunday afternoon, and he wanted Adila and me to come in the morning to practice. My sister and I told him we could not come as we were going to church.

"Would you pray for me then?" he asked.

We did, and he won the competition. Doors began to open for him professionally, and because of seeing our prayers answered, his heart opened to Jesus, and he started attending church. It was a long process, but as he gave his heart to Jesus bit by bit and received God's love in exchange, his life completely changed. He is now happily married to a woman and has children.

All the models and designers we worked with were Muslim and had never heard of the love of Jesus. Many of them came to our home congregation in a friend's house as it was easier for them to come to someone's house than to go to a church building. One day we showed them *The Passion of Christ* movie, and they were in tears as they understood what Jesus had done for them. Many gave their hearts to the Lord that night.

Our home congregation was my very favorite time of the week. We had twenty to thirty young people, many of them

Muslim, and we were able to read the Bible, pray and worship. It was like the first church talked about in Acts 2:46–47 (NIV):

> They broke bread in their homes and ate together with glad and sincere hearts, praising God and enjoying the favor of all the people. And the Lord added to their number daily those who were being saved.

I learned that God can use us wherever we are; where you are placed is your mission field. For a time my mission field was the fashion and modeling world. My sister Malika later joined us as a model, and I worked on and off for about three years. It was amazing, unexpected provision.

Immediate Answers

One day in the spring I was walking to Bible school and had $100 in my pocket. But when I arrived and put my hand in my pocket, the money had vanished. I searched everywhere, checking all my pockets over and over and emptying the contents of my bag. However, my money was gone.

"What's wrong?" asked a friend, seeing my frantic search.

"I've lost $100," I said hopelessly.

To encourage me, he told me the story of a friend who had lost her purse with a lot of money in it on a bus in Europe. She prayed, reminding God that she had been faithful with her money, always tithing, and asked Him to return what the locust had stolen.

The next day she got back on the same bus and, miraculously, there right in front of her was her wallet, with all the money inside it. Another friend, Taliba, meaning "Seeker of knowledge," told me her ID had been stolen in Europe. She had prayed, and the next day it was delivered to her mailbox. She believed angels had brought it back.

A similar thing had happened to Adila. She was at Bible school living in Europe at the time. One cold January evening she was making her way home. It was the middle of winter with deep snow on the ground. As she put her hand in her pocket to reach for her key, it wasn't there. She had lost it, and there were no spares. Adila cried out to the God who sees and knows, asking Him to show her where the key was. Mounds of fresh snow were all around her, but Adila immediately had a sense of where the key was. In faith she took a shovel, and the first spadeful of snow uncovered her room key. She was amazed and rejoiced at God's immediate answer to her prayer, praising Him that He is close to those in need.

My faith was stirred up. I knew if He could do it for them, He could do it for me. I started praying for a word of knowledge so I would know where to look. Later that day, as I was praying in the Spirit, the Lord gave me a picture of where the money was. I walked the exact same way I had traveled, and when I got to the busiest part, there right in front of me was my $100 bill on the ground. I knew it was a miracle as it was in the middle of a very busy road near the market, between a school and a hospital, and it had been raining all day. Rejoicing, I ran to Bible school to share the good news.

Giving It Away

I was very involved in church, serving in the worship team. I also led a home congregation and taught the dance team. I was employed full-time at the church as a translator and youth leader until I got a job teaching my language to diplomats from the American Embassy. My modeling continued on the side, and I also worked as a beautician. Even though I was not working full-time for the church anymore, I still served in hospitality. I would welcome international visitors and help find houses and apartments for people staying in the city.

It was through the job of finding apartments that I became a real estate agent. God's favor was on me, and once more I quickly became very successful, so much so that I was able to use my income to support my family. When I had my first month's salary, I felt God tell me to give it all away as a first-fruits offering. Like the first fruit from a harvest, the salary was

> I felt God tell me to give it all away as a first-fruits offering. "Give it all away?" I asked, incredulous.

my first harvest from my work, and giving it all away was an acknowledgment that all I had was from Him.

But I didn't find it easy. "Give it *all* away?" I asked, incredulous.

I was sure that I hadn't heard correctly and at first tried to ignore the thought. I did not obey the Lord the first month and, sure enough, where I was prospering once, the blessing suddenly stopped. There was a block in my work, and I knew it was my disobedience toward God.

"You need to obey Me. This is My money," God said when I went back to Him in prayer.

I was convicted and asked His forgiveness for not obeying straightaway.

I had to trust Him with the provision He had given me, so I decided to give my entire month's salary to my church. As I handed the cash to my pastor, he was shocked at the sum and looked from the cash to me with surprise.

"It's not a mistake; this is what I want to give!" I said, laughing.

I was so full of joy. The freedom that comes from obedience is amazing. By obeying Him, I put my trust back into God's hands instead of in riches.

As my father could no longer work because of his accident, we were all doing what we could to put food on the table and pay for our bills. In our culture it is expected that the children help support their parents. The elderly are never put in old people's homes but are the most honored in our culture. Muqaddas had set up a cleaning company. Iman was working as a barista. Malika was making and selling dresses. Dawud was doing construction and remodeling work. My older brothers were busy supporting their own families, and Adila had gone back to another Bible school in Europe.

After the war, our apartment was in great need of repair. The rooms were barely habitable with no glass in the windows and no furniture. We'd had to sell all of our possessions to buy food, and anything we did have left was broken and old. My sisters, brother and I used to walk from room to room, asking God for the things we needed. Faith has a voice, and we knew that God was our supply, so we spoke out our praises at His provision before we had received anything. In the kitchen, we laid hands on our broken fridge, thanking God for a new one.

> Faith has a voice, and we knew that God was our supply, so we spoke out our praises at His provision before we had received anything.

We thanked Him that He would supply our needs, and He always did. Sometimes it was through a house selling and the owners getting rid of furniture and appliances. Other times it was through being blessed in our work so that we could buy new things. Yet, through it all, His timing was perfect.

Suleyman's Story

In the midst of all my work there was heartbreak in the family. My brother Suleyman was dying from tuberculosis (TB). He had first become ill when he was in the army during the civil war.

It was the middle of winter, thick snow was on the ground and Suleyman was the commander of a troop of young men who were on patrol in the countryside. They were marching through a field when shooting started.

My brother realized his men were surrounded. All they could do was run for whatever cover they could find. Suleyman pushed himself into a small hole in the ground, then covered himself with as much snow as he could. Many of his men were killed, but even though a tank drove over the snow above Suleyman, he survived.

After what seemed like hours of waiting for the all-clear, my brother, now freezing and coughing, squeezed himself out of the hole. Only twenty men survived, and once they had found each other, they tried to scramble up the side of the mountain. There were deep caves in the rock face, and they were able to find refuge.

However, the enemy was close by and had seen them moving up the mountainside. A battle commenced, and it went on for days. The weather remained bitterly cold, and Suleyman and his men had no food. They eventually ran out of bullets, too. Suleyman knew he had to get more ammunition, so when it was dark, he crawled along the ground into no-man's land and picked up used bullets to re-use. He risked his life for his men, but he had no other choice. In the daylight Suleyman and his men could see the enemy torturing their victims, cutting their bodies into pieces, trying to sow fear into my brother and the other soldiers.

Eventually, after two weeks of hiding in the cave, braving the cold, Suleyman and his men were rescued when more soldiers arrived. By the time we found out what had happened, Suleyman was receiving medical attention. Even though his life had been spared, he had contracted TB. He was broken by what he had been through but also stunned that he had survived. I knew without a doubt that God had spared his life because of our prayers.

During the war, Adila, Malika and I would fast and pray for God to save his life. Upon his return, we continued to pray for his healing, but he was very weak. Since becoming ill, he had found it hard to hold down a job as he was in and out of the hospital so often. He moved to Europe for a time to try to find work but had to return home because the cold weather there was so detrimental to his health.

God had spared his life because of our prayers.

When I started working as a real estate agent, a few years after the war ended, Suleyman took a turn for the worse.

"There is no hope for him. He is not responding to the medicine and doesn't have long to live," the doctor told my father.

Mama cried as she understood what the doctor's words meant.

Suleyman was married with two children and was sent home to be cared for by his wife as the hospital said there was nothing more they could do. Suleyman lived about thirty minutes from our house, and my mother was constantly at his bedside caring for him. When I went to see him, I was shocked. He was a ghost of the man he used to be. But I was determined. My brother was not yet a Christian, and I was going to fight in prayer for his life.

My family and I fasted and prayed in Jesus' name for our brother. I knew it was not God's will for Suleyman to go in this way. God had saved his life once; I knew He could do it again.

As I was praying, I heard the voice of God.

"I want you to tithe 90 percent of your income."

I knew it had to be God. I'd never have thought of that myself; it seemed crazy. "How can I live on 10 percent?" I asked, knowing it would not be enough to cover my expenses.

As I waited to hear more, I felt God show me that it was an act of faith and that He was going to bless my obedience. I asked for confirmation that this word was from Him. The Lord reminded me of the parable of the lost sheep, when the good

Shepherd left the 99 and went for the 1 lost. It was a sign to me to give 90 percent and live on 10 percent.

That Sunday in the sermon the pastor spoke about tithing 90 percent. It was the first time I had ever heard him talk about it, and the last. I knew that indeed God was speaking, and this time I quickly and willingly obeyed. I began to tithe 90 percent instead of 10 percent each month, worshiping Jesus with my finances. It became a lifestyle, and immediately there was fruit.

Suleyman was completely and miraculously healed. He listened when we told him that Jesus was his healer, and that was why he was better, but Suleyman still did not yet choose to follow Jesus.

Giving the 90 percent of my salary was a breakthrough for me in giving extravagantly to the Lord

> **As I was praying, I heard the voice of God. "I want you to tithe 90 percent of your income."**

and His Kingdom. It was so joyful. After that episode I became more and more successful in my work, so much so that I was soon the top real estate agent in my city, overtaking those who had been building up their businesses over many years. The Lord supplied a seed for me to sow, and He multiplied the harvest.

> The point is this: whoever sows sparingly will also reap sparingly, and whoever sows bountifully will also reap bountifully. Each one must give as he has decided in his heart, not reluctantly or under compulsion, for God loves a cheerful giver. And God is able to make all grace abound to you, so that having all sufficiency in all things at all times, you may abound in every good work. As it is written, "He has distributed freely, he has given to the poor; his righteousness endures forever." He who supplies seed to the sower and bread for food will supply and multiply your seed for sowing and increase the harvest of your righteousness.
>
> 2 Corinthians 9:6–10 ESV

People asked me what my secret was; they wanted me to train them. I ended up working with three girls, making them my disciples. God was showing me I could take every opportunity to make disciples and that I should not despise the day of small beginnings (see Zechariah 4:10). I was doing so well, and God was prospering me, that the 10 percent I was living on was more than enough. Now God had me influencing another sphere—the sphere of economy.

At that time our church wanted to buy land for a new building. I had read about how David had given money to build a house for the Lord before he built his own mansion. Solomon had built the Temple of the Lord before his own home, and the prophet Haggai chastised the Israelites for building their own houses before restoring the Temple. I felt God challenging me to give to Him before I bought my own home.

During that time I had sold an apartment as part of my real estate business. My commission was 2 percent, but the owner was so generous that, as a thank-you, he gave me 3 percent, which was about $5,000. This was a lot of money, and my family and I could have made good use of it. However, I decided to give it all away to the church. It wasn't easy, and I struggled to let the money go with joy. But the more I gave, the more I reaped hundredfold and more overflowing. When I gave God that $5,000, after a while He blessed me back with about $50,000!

God is no man's debtor and is always faithful when we obey. I was learning firsthand the reality of Malachi 3:10:

> "Bring the whole tithe into the storehouse, so that there may be food in My house, and test Me now in this," says the LORD of hosts, "if I will not open for you the windows of heaven and pour out for you a blessing until it overflows."

We can never out-give God. He gave everything—even His own precious Son.

24

GO TO THE END OF THE EARTH

Acts 1:8 tells us, "You will receive power when the Holy Spirit comes on you; and you will be my witnesses in Jerusalem, and in all Judea and Samaria, and to the ends of the earth" (NIV).

To stand before the King of kings left me with the certainty that heaven and eternity is the true reality. Jesus was and is the Source of all light and the darkness cannot prevail over Him.

From that time forth in my life, when I prayed, "Thy kingdom come, Thy will be done" (Matthew 6:10 KJV), I knew that His Kingdom already existed and that His will would be done. Nothing can stop the fulfillment of all prophecy.

I no longer had any fear of death. If God is for us who can be against us? As Romans 8:35–39 (NIV) says:

Who shall separate us from the love of Christ? Shall trouble or hardship or persecution or famine or nakedness or danger or sword? As it is written: "For your sake we face death all day long; we are considered as sheep to be slaughtered." No, in all these things we are more than conquerors through him who loved us. For I am convinced that neither death nor life, neither angels nor demons, neither the present nor the future, nor any powers, neither height nor depth, nor anything else in all creation, will be able to separate us from the love of God that is in Christ Jesus our Lord.

My sisters also embraced the boldness to live fearlessly for Jesus Christ, our good Shepherd. By His great love, we were sent to seek the lost sheep of this world. Adila and I felt a deep compassion and calling to reach out to other Muslims with the Good News. We were emboldened by the Great Commission in Matthew 28:19–20 (NKJV):

"Go therefore and make disciples of all the nations, baptizing them in the name of the Father and of the Son and of the Holy Spirit, teaching them to observe all things that I have commanded you; and lo, I am with you always, *even* to the end of the age."

Journey into Danger

After I spoke to a group of missionary students, they were challenged and called by the Lord to go to the most dangerous Islamic country practicing Sharia Law. It was not a journey to be undertaken lightly. The craggy mountains are among the most remote, most dangerous places in the world.

With Adila as translator, the team set out for shepherd camps in the high country canyons in order to reach people who could not even read and had never heard the Gospel. The company was armed with audio Bibles translated into their language and the *Jesus* film, which would be shown with the help of a solar-powered projector in villages throughout the mountains.

Adila and the others traveled by horseback for many days to reach the spring camps of nomadic shepherds.

All went smoothly as the truth of the Gospel was embraced by those who watched the *Jesus* film. Sometimes 150 or even two hundred men, women and children would gather to meet and experience the claims of Jesus the Messiah. Many of the Muslim shepherds received Christ on the journey and danced in joy to a song about the wedding day. It was so profound and and also prophetic of the wedding day the Father is preparing for His Son.

After many days had passed, warning came from a villager that the team had one day to leave the country before the jihadists would capture, torture and kill them.

Many intercessors, including myself, were praying for their safety all that time. The Lord heard us in our distress and kept them alive.

Adila told me later she felt no fear as they escaped from those who were dedicated to the slaughter of all infidels in the name of Allah. The God of Abraham, Isaac and Jacob was with them! Jesus had put a host of angels around the team, and they were evacuated safely. That the threat was real and the warning justified was confirmed when the next missionaries to visit the same region were slaughtered by jihadist forces.

Being unafraid to die does not mean that the moment of crossing into eternity may not exist behind the next boulder or just around the next bend in a narrow trail. It means living each moment so that it counts for eternity.

It means, as Matthew 22:37–40 says, to love God first, and then to love our neighbor as ourselves.

As for me, I had the certainty and faith that if I died, I would once again stand before my Lord and would hear Him say, "Well done, good and faithful servant!"

There have been some times since my visit to heaven that I can't wait to go there again. I know for certain that when I see Him again, I will never leave His presence.

25

GOING TO AMERICA

My desire to go to the USA in order to study grew. I was inspired by the book of Daniel in the Bible. Daniel was a man of influence because of his education, and I wanted to have the best education in order to impact the world for Jesus. I knew that Hosea 4:6 (NIV) says, "My people are destroyed from lack of knowledge," so I made it my quest to seek knowledge and wisdom in order to be best used by the Lord. I did not want to study in my country as the colleges were either Muslim or secular. My dream was to go to a Christian college.

Almost ten years previously, my friends had gone on a month-long mission trip to America.

When they returned, my friends told me stories of what America was like. They traveled to different churches ministering and giving presentations. It had been a childhood dream of mine to go to America, and they had gone, but I had not! In God's timing, though, I felt that one day I would go.

I continued to learn English by reading books, especially an English Bible, and practicing with foreigners in order to prepare me for a time in the future when, with God's leading, I would go and study in America. I thought about asking some Americans I knew for help and advice, but nothing I tried worked out.

As I prayed, the Lord revealed to me that He alone was going to send me and that I needed to trust Him. He showed me I did not need to hope in a person to get me to America. God was teaching me to depend on Him and no one else. In no man but God alone I put my trust.

Building on Faith

Adila was given a book for her birthday about a man who had built a university by faith. I borrowed it, read it and then again read Luke 18:27: "What is impossible with man is possible with God" (NIV). The words made a huge impact on me, and I began to believe them for my own life.

When I went to a conference in Europe with my church, I heard about that university once more because it had an affiliate university in Europe. I started praying about whether I should apply and sent for a brochure.

Then something else extraordinary happened. When I'd gone to heaven, Jesus had told me not to speak about what had happened for a period of time. The experience was sacred, and I hadn't yet been given permission to release it. Although I was bursting to tell people, I had to wait for the appointed time. Like Mary, when she was pregnant with Jesus, and Elizabeth with John, there was a season of being hidden before a season of openness. I knew I had to be obedient. Later, I realized that I'd needed time to process such a huge experience and let the reality sink in.

It would be five years before I could talk about my heavenly experience. But at that conference in Europe, the Lord released me to share my story about the bomb, going to heaven and meeting Jesus face to face. I just had to close my eyes to remember the awe and wonder I'd felt and fell to the ground weeping. I felt God say, "Now it is time for you to speak worldwide, to wake up the Church."

My story was first told to the conference in Europe. The bomb and the persecution had been like a refining fire in my life. The reward was seeing Jesus in His majesty and glory. People often tell me that they want to see Jesus face to face like I did, but they do not realize that the cost is their life. As God said to Moses, "You cannot see my face, for no one may see me and live" (Exodus 33:20 NIV). I saw Jesus in death, and He raised me to life.

> If we open our eyes, we can see Jesus in each other.

I believe that, if we open our eyes, we can see Jesus in each other. After all, we each carry His treasure—the Holy Spirit. But I'm convinced it's greater to not have seen Jesus face to face and still believe, as He said in John 20:29: "Blessed are they who did not see, and yet believed."

When I got back home, I called the university with the help of a friend and asked if it was possible to study there. They said I had to pass an English test before I could be considered. I knew my English was not good enough, so I started looking at language courses.

Faith Can Move Mountains

A friend of mine who graduated from the same U.S. university I wanted to attend and was a missionary in my country told me about a mission organization that did courses for English as a Second Language (ESL). I liked the word *mission,* as I knew Jesus was a missionary who came from heaven to earth, and I wanted to be like Jesus. When another person told me about the same organization, I decided to look into it and applied with the help of my friend Shakila. At that time I had no idea that I was applying to a worldwide organization that had a university in America. I wanted to do an ESL, but I was told that I needed to do a discipleship school first, which would be three months of biblical teaching and then two and a half months of practical outreach. I later found out that someone had made a mistake. Actually, this was the opposite of what is normally required.

The fees for the school and my travel would cost thousands of dollars, and I didn't have any money. But God responds to faith when you believe He performs miracles. Faith pleases God, and faith can move mountains.

I felt I had to make a decision in faith and the money would come in. To boost my faith, I began singing the lyrics to a Don Moen song: "God will make a way, where there seems to be no way. . . ."

> **God responds to faith when you believe He performs miracles.**

I also declared the verse in Revelation 3:7: "What he opens no one can shut, and what he shuts no one can open" (NIV).

It wasn't long before I heard I would be able to pay reduced fees for the school because I was from a Third World country. This encouraged me, and I had an assurance that God was opening the door for me. However, when I told my parents about my plans, they did not give me their blessing to go.

"No, you can study here in this country," they both said.

"God told me to go," I insisted, but they would not be moved.

I tried to persuade them. They knew my dream but were afraid that they would never see me again. In tears I begged for their release and blessing, but they were adamant that I had to stay.

In my culture it is expected for a girl to only leave her family home when she gets married.

My parents had said no, and I knew I had to honor and obey them. Of all the Ten Commandments in Exodus, the fifth commandment is the only one with a blessing attached: "Honor your father and your mother, so that you may live long in the land the LORD your God is giving you" (20:12 NIV).

> My parents had said no, and I knew I had to honor and obey them.

The Lord said I must not leave without their blessing. Over the next months I cried out to God day and night, praying and fasting, and continually asked my parents if they would release me.

"Wait and be patient and I will change their hearts," said the Lord.

I had to wait a whole year before they finally released me to go to the school. God told me it was the right time, and when I asked again, both my mother and father relented and said I could go.

For the previous year I had been telling people that I was going to America. They laughed and ridiculed me, saying, "Why are you still here then?"

But I knew that I was speaking prophetically that I would go. As Jesus said in Mark 11:23 (NIV):

"If anyone says to this mountain, 'Go, throw yourself into the sea,' and does not doubt in their heart but believes that what they say will happen, it will be done for them."

Indeed faith has power and a voice.

However, I still did not have money or a visa. "Lord, what should I do?" I asked.

A friend told me to talk to the pastor of the international church. I knew it was a divine appointment. He was a missionary from America and asked me to share my testimony with his family. Then he shared my story at his church. After the service he and his wife blessed me with $600.

"What should I do now, Lord?" I asked again.

"Get a visa and go," came the reply to my heart.

It all seemed impossible. An interview with the American Embassy for a visa had to be made three months in advance. It was then only a few days before Christmas, and the school started at the beginning of January.

My friend Shakila called the consul to ask what I should do. She passed the phone over to me.

"Come on January 11 after the holidays for an interview," the consul said.

"That's too late!" I cried. I needed to be in America then.

He said there was nothing he could do.

Very disheartened, I put down the phone. How was God going to accomplish this?

I decided to pray and fast. My sisters and our home congregation joined me.

Iman worked at a café in our city at the time. She had a colleague there who was friends with the consul. She called on my behalf, and then I talked to him. This time he said I could come in the next day. I had gotten in by the skin of my teeth, as it was just a few days before Christmas.

Indeed faith has power and a voice.

The Lord had changed his heart.

I arrived at the embassy excited and nervous at the same time. I was interviewed and asked what I would be doing in America.

"I'm doing a course at a mission school and then going on outreach," I replied.

"You're so lucky," the man said in a friendly tone. "That area is supposed to be very beautiful. Where are you going on outreach?"

"I don't know. I will pray about it," I replied.

"You should go to Asia," he said.

I smiled, sure that he must be a Christian and that God had placed him there to open the way for me.

My passport was stamped, and I was given a yearlong visa. It was a miracle. It was hard to get a visa to the United States from a Muslim country because of the fear of terrorism, especially after the 9/11 tragedy. Friends had told me that it was also very hard for single young girls to get visas. I had none of the prerequisites for a visa—no ticket and not enough money—but I was never asked about those details.

With my $100 visa in hand, I jubilantly left the consul. The $500 I had remaining was enough to fly to Europe, and then I would get another flight to the USA.

It was New Year's, and I stayed with Malika and Adila, who were at a Bible school. This was Adila's second time at Bible school in Europe. The first time she had been at the one connected to our church.

I felt strongly I should not go back. I could only go forward.

I called the mission organization in America to tell them I was coming but found out that there had been a mix-up and they weren't expecting me.

"There's no space. Come next quarter," they said.

What could I do? When I prayed, I felt strongly I should not go back. I could only go forward.

"Go, and I will be with you," God said.

So I obeyed, but I still had no money. As I was praying, I felt God prompt me to ask two friends to borrow $1,000 each. I struggled with this, as I would have preferred not to be in debt. But they gladly loaned me the money, and it was enough to get me to Los Angeles.

Culture Shock

Arriving at the busy LAX airport, my first time on American soil, I felt so alone in the huge terminal. I had never traveled by myself before, and it was such a culture shock. Everything was so different from my homeland. I didn't have a way to get to the school. I didn't know anyone in America, and I didn't know what to do.

But God did.

I was crying as I walked around the airport. Eventually, exhausted, I went to sleep on a chair. After a while I woke up, still tired and now

When we take one step toward Him, He takes a hundred steps toward us.

aching from the uncomfortable seat. I immediately started to pray, and as I did so, I felt God tell me I was not alone. He was with me.

Peace filled my heart, and I asked Him what to do next.

I already knew He responded to faith and that, when we take one step toward Him, He takes a hundred steps toward us. We do the possible, and He does the impossible.

Suddenly I noticed a young woman sitting near me reading a book. She was in her twenties with blond, curly hair and blue eyes.

"Ask for her help," the Lord prompted me.

Okay, Lord! I told Him in my thoughts. A little nervous, I walked over to approach her. "Excuse me. May I ask you a favor? Could you please help me?" I asked as politely as possible.

She was immediately open and friendly, telling me she was a missionary's daughter.

I said I needed to find cheap tickets online. She didn't have a laptop, but we found a place to get on the Internet at the airport, and she showed me how to get a ticket cheaply online.

Then she said: "God has put it in my heart to bless you" and gave me the money to pay for it. I was amazed. She didn't even know me, yet she showed me the generosity of Jesus.

Later I wondered if she was an angel—or maybe even better, a saint. I tried to contact her after I arrived at the school but never heard back. I knew the Lord had demonstrated another tremendous truth: Wherever He leads me, He provides for my needs. When it is God's will, it's God's bill!

Arriving at the School

A few hours later I arrived at my final destination. Filled with excitement, and somehow not so tired anymore, I breathed deeply of the warm air and noted the lush vegetation. As I found a taxi to take me to the school, memories flooded in of the cold nights at home when Adila and I waited in long lines for food.

I was carried back to one particular winter's evening during the war. Adila and I were in the queue, waiting for the promise of food. We couldn't go home with empty hands, but it was getting dark and cold. A gentle sprinkling of snow began to fall. We shivered together, huddling close, trying to keep each other warm from the blasts of Arctic air. If we left the line we would lose our place and miss our chance for something to eat. We had no choice but to stay.

"I'm so cold," murmured Adila, her blue lips covering her chattering teeth.

"I'm not cold," I said defiantly to the frosty weather. "I'm on a warm, balmy island!"

"What?" said my sister, laughing at my joke.

I pictured the hot sun in the blue sky and pretended it was warming my face. My make-believe game helped us through the night. Each time we stamped our feet to keep the blood moving, I said we were on a beautiful beach, stamping on the golden sand, instead of freezing snow.

However much I imagined I was in a warm, lush place, harsh reality had a habit of banishing my little dreams away.

Now, here I was—in a warm, balmy place, just like I'd envisioned. What I had spoken had become reality, similar to how the Lord spoke all creation into being. It struck me that there is power in our tongues and that I should speak out in faith—blessings, not curses; life, not death.

Arriving on the campus a few miles from the airport, I couldn't help laughing with joy. The taxi pulled up at the gate and I was asked what I was doing at the university.

"I'm a student. I am doing a discipleship school!" I replied.

"Which one?" the lady asked.

I didn't know, but God had already spoken to me about going to Asia after reading the letter to the churches in Asia in Revelation, so I said, "Asia discipleship school." I learned later that the leaders of the

> **Here I was— in a warm, balmy place, just like I'd envisioned.**

school had just changed the name to Asia Discipleship School. I didn't have a clue, but God knew!

My leaders were surprised to see me but welcomed me anyway, and a space was miraculously found. Even though it was late evening by this time, they found some sheets for my bed.

"Are you hungry?" they asked as they walked me to my room.

I felt my stomach rumble. I had fasted for the three days of my journey because God had told me to fast until I got to the school. Now that I could eat, I happily munched a pizza with the leaders and, between mouthfuls, told them my story.

A few hours later, as I lay in my bunk, sharing a room with seven other girls, I was overwhelmed by God's provision. He was my faithful Provider. I was in America.

God had made a way when the way seemed impossible.

Abundant Miracles

During my time at the school the Lord woke me every morning at 3:00 and 4:00 a.m. to spend time with Him. I would creep out of bed so as to not wake my roommates and run to the prayer room on the grounds for an hour of conversation with Him. I was so hungry for the presence of God.

I shared my testimony with the school, and many of the students and staff were moved. They gave me a love offering, and I was not only able to pay off my $2,000 debt but also pay my school fees and outreach fees in full. I was so touched at the faithfulness of God and the generosity of the Body of Christ.

When I sent the money to my friends in Europe, they were shocked at how quickly I had been able to pay them back.

No one from home believed I had actually made it to America. The winter of that year was the worst winter in my country for many years, so my friends joked that I had picked a good time to go somewhere warm!

After I told my my story, I found out these people—and other prayer warriors and missionaries from all over the world—had been praying for me and my nation, for our salvation. I was the answer to their prayers! They had prayed, too, when they heard about the bomb.

I met a missionary from New Zealand who told me that as soon as he heard about the explosion, and that people were badly injured and in the hospital, he began praying for us. I also met an American man and woman who said the same thing. I was so encouraged because I knew their prayers had made a difference.

I learned something else. When I shared my testimony with Muslims, they had dreams and visitations from Jesus. And, usually, after I told about my story and the love of Jesus, a sign from heaven followed, as described in Acts. Most of the time it rained . . . and sometimes, even in late spring, it snowed.

Ministering in Asia

I ended up going to southeast Asia on an extended six-month practical outreach after the lecture phase. God did many miracles. He provided all of the money that I needed, showing me that He is faithful beyond my imagination.

God did many miracles.

I was able to teach tae kwon do while I preached the Gospel in southeast Asia. I also went into female prisons to teach haircutting as I shared about God's love. I spent time with murderers and prostitutes but did not judge. I simply loved them, like Jesus would.

We went to a military hospital in southeast Asia. A man there was dying from AIDS. We laid hands on him and prayed for his healing in Jesus' name. Over time he was healed. Now he goes to the hospital to pray for the sick instead of being treated himself.

At an orphanage in southeast Asia there were many sick children. After experiencing the suffering I have, I can feel the pain of suffering people and desire to comfort them, just as Jesus was moved to compassion and healed all who were sick or suffered. I loved playing with the children and let them clamber all over me, kissing and hugging them. I noticed a few of them had small scars but guessed they were from mosquito bites so didn't think too much about it. I was teaching them hip-hop dancing and was exhausted by the end of the day. The heat was intense, sapping me of energy.

A few days later I began to develop a fever and felt dizzy and nauseous.

"You stay in bed and rest today," said our group leader.

I was too weak to reply and just closed my eyes as beads of sweat trickled down my face. My skin was starting to itch, and very quickly red welts sprang up on my body. None of us knew what was wrong, so I was taken to the hospital.

There a doctor diagnosed chicken pox. Suddenly I realized what the scars were on the children I had been playing with. They had chicken pox and, never having it as a child, I had caught it. There were ten people in our team, but I was the only one who came down with the virus, as all the others were immune. Later my outreach leader told me the doctor had said someone my age could die from the chicken pox. But they prayed for my life and my healing. Jesus, the best Physician, healed me.

Many invited Jesus into their hearts.

For ten days I suffered, my skin itching so much it brought me to tears. By a miracle I had strength not to scratch, so my chicken pox left no lasting scars.

When I got better, I went straight back to help at the orphanage. I would lay hands on the orphans in their little cots, interceding for their lives. When I came to one tiny boy, I was shocked at the sight of him. He was a bag of bones; there was barely any flesh on his body. He was so sick they didn't think he would make it.

In the days after we prayed he began to gain weight. Eventually he became the chubbiest baby and was completely healed, then adopted by a family. Many, many other children were also healed.

One boy, a Buddhist with whom I had shared my story, had a nightmare. He was terrified, being pursued by evil spirits. Suddenly he saw a light and heard my voice calling him. As he turned to see me, he saw the face of Jesus instead. When he awoke, he gave his life to Christ. I was amazed when I heard this story. I knew Jesus was revealing Himself in dreams to many Muslims, but this was the first time I knew He also revealed Himself to a Buddhist by a dream.

The most healing miracles Jesus performed when I prayed were the moms who hadn't had babies for a long time and miraculously conceived babies.

I also gave my testimony to a group of prostitutes and sex-trafficked women and children in southeast Asia. They cried as I told my story, and many invited Jesus into their hearts.

It was such an honor to be used by Jesus this way.

I wanted to live a life worthy of His calling. God had brought me back to live for Him, to tell the world that Jesus is alive and that we must prepare a way for the Second Coming. I longed to live every single day like it was my last day.

More Bible School

After my school was completed, I felt God tell me to do more Bible training before I started any other ministry. Then I would be ready to equip others with His Word of truth. As John 8:32 says, "Then you will know the truth, and the truth will set you free" (NIV). I wanted to immerse myself in that truth.

I loved the story of Mary and Martha and pondered what Jesus had said to Martha: "Mary has chosen what is better, and it will not be taken away from her" (Luke 10:42 NIV). He was asking Martha to choose the better way—spending time at His feet listening to His Word, which is sweet as honey.

After finishing Bible school in a warm part of America, I moved to a cold part of America where the Lord led me and told me to do a worship school and learn the skills to worship Him in spirit and in truth. Since worship in heaven is nonstop,

God impressed it upon me that He wants it also to be like that on earth, because He is worthy of praise. I live to worship Him, so when He opens a door, I walk through. He then makes a way again by miraculously providing, as my good Shepherd, so that I don't lack anything (see Psalm 23).

As I was used to warm climates, the thought of a cold winter with snow seemed something I could not bear. I prayed that it would not snow . . . and the Lord answered my prayer! It didn't snow. That was the warmest winter anyone had witnessed. Just as Elijah, an ordinary man, prayed that it wouldn't rain and it did not rain, I knew that prayer was powerful.

Then the next year the drought was bad, and I thought about the farmers, who needed the moisture from the snow for a good harvest. I realized that the snow was indeed a blessing. So, that second year, I prayed that it would snow. The Lord answered again. The winter was cold, and it snowed so much that snow fell even in April and May.

When the Lord led me to share my story at this worship school, many who heard it invited me to share it with their families. One woman's husband was a doctor I had met previously when he had come to my country on a medical mission. Their church adopted

Revelation is like the pearl; wisdom is the treasure.

our country and for years prayed for us and sent missionaries.

School was very challenging for me, as it was intense study and lectures, but God gave me many revelations through His Word. Revelation is like the pearl; wisdom is the treasure.

Some of the things I was learning was to worship in spirit and in truth, to sing the Word of God from my heart straight to the heart of God and to write new songs for Jesus. I began to sing my prayers, as commanded in Zephaniah 3:14–17. As the Lord sings over me, I sing over Him, and His Word unlocks my heart and makes it alive.

Fasting As a Lifestyle

Every New Year I ask God how He wants me to fast for that year. Last year I fasted for three days each month. This year I fasted for forty days at the beginning of the year. The next year I will fast for the first ten days of the year, then every week for two days and the first three days of each month. Fasting has become a lifestyle as a believer. I believe it helps me hear God's voice clearly, keeps my heart tender and brings breakthrough.

On outreach in southeast Asia in August, I had a dream of the Second Coming of Jesus. I saw Judgment Day as described in the book of Revelation. It was terrifying—like watching a scene from Noah's Ark where the flood destroyed everything.

My dream showed the world living "as it was in the days of Noah" (Matthew 24:37 NIV)—everyone eating, drinking and getting married. Jesus came suddenly, like a thief in the night, to take His Church, His Bride. I was sweating and trembling when I awoke. Jesus told me to get ready because He is coming soon. When I woke, I recalled 1 Thessalonians 4:16–18:

> For the Lord Himself will descend from heaven with a shout, with the voice of the archangel and with the trumpet of God, and the dead in Christ will rise first. Then we who are alive and remain will be caught up together with them in the clouds to meet the Lord in the air, and so we shall always be with the Lord. Therefore comfort one another with these words.

In the beginning of doing the Bible course, the Lord asked me to fast for forty days, consuming only juice and water. During that time, I asked Him to reveal the secrets of His heart to me. He gave me another dream, and this time I woke feeling peaceful. Jesus appeared to me as the Prince of Peace, the Victorious One, arriving to take His Bride. He appeared, wearing a white robe and mounted on a white horse, with chariots of fire in a cloud of glory, coming in the clouds. It was a beautiful picture of Revelation 1:7:

> Behold, He is coming with the clouds, and every eye will see Him, even those who pierced Him; and all the tribes of the earth will mourn over Him. So it is to be. Amen.

The message was the same as before: "My Bride, get ready. I'm coming soon." "Watch therefore, and pray always that you may be counted worthy to escape all these things that will come to pass, and to stand before the Son of Man" (Luke 21:36 NKJV).

Epilogue

Four Dreams

During Rosh Hashanah (Jewish New Year) I had just come out of a Daniel fast—eating only vegetables and drinking water. One morning I was reading Luke chapter four, about Jesus fasting in the desert at the start of His ministry.

"Will you do the same?" I felt the Lord ask. "I want you to fast like I did, but only drink water."

Jesus had fasted for forty days when He was thirty years old and then was filled with the *power* of the Holy Spirit. He is the highest example for me. I was now thirty, and I wanted to fast for the power of the Holy Spirit in my life as well. However, I had never given up all food and juices, everything but water before, and I didn't know if I could do it. But God was in control, and I found out later that a Daniel fast is a perfect preparation for a full fast. The Lord had been preparing my body before I even knew what He was asking of me.

During the fast I had four dreams: one in the middle and the last three at the end of the forty days.

The First Dream: Bread of Life

In this first very vivid dream Jesus came to me as the Bread of Life. I was given the most delicious, satisfying bread I could imagine. I took a bite. Never had I tasted anything so good! It was a reddish-brown Middle Eastern loaf, huge and freshly baked. It was so good that I didn't want to wake up from the dream, as one bite from the bread satisfied my hunger.

Two verses came to mind:

"Man shall not live by bread alone, but by every word that proceeds from the mouth of God."

Matthew 4:4 NKJV

"Truly, truly, I say to you, it is not Moses who has given you the bread out of heaven, but it is My Father who gives you the true bread out of heaven. For the bread of God is that which comes down out of heaven, and gives life to the world." Then they said to Him, "Lord, always give us this bread." Jesus said to them, "I am the bread of life; he who comes to Me will not hunger, and he who believes in Me will never thirst. But I said to you that you have seen Me, and yet do not believe. All that the Father gives Me will come to Me, and the one who comes to Me I will certainly not cast out. For I have come down from heaven, not to do My own will, but the will of Him who sent Me. This is the will of Him who sent Me, that of all that He has given Me I lose nothing, but raise it up on the last day. For this is the will of My Father, that everyone who beholds the Son and believes in Him will have eternal life, and I Myself will raise him up on the last day."

John 6:32–40

When I woke, it was as if I had eaten a full meal. I asked the Lord what He was saying through the dream.

He told me, "I am the bread of heaven. When you eat of Me, you will be truly satisfied. My Word brings life. Taste and see that I am good. Eat the scroll."

I was reminded of Deuteronomy 8:16: "He gave you manna to eat in the wilderness" (NIV). God was giving me manna from heaven to feast on. After the dream, when I smelled food I felt ill, instead of being hungry for it. The bread in my dream carried me through the fast.

It was common for me to have dreams when I was fasting, but I never spoke about them right away. I would wait and ask the Holy Spirit for the interpretation. I needed confirmation to know if the dream was just for me, or whether the Lord wanted me to share with others.

The Second Dream: Double Portion of the Bread of Life

Near the end of my forty days I had the second dream. It confirmed what God had already shown me in the first dream. This time there were two pieces of bread—a double portion. I felt God was reminding me that two is better than one, and the marriage of the Bride and the Lamb is coming. I understood that the Lord is preparing a wedding. He started in the beginning of time with a wedding, creating family in Genesis, and Revelation ends with a wedding. Also, Jesus' first miracle (John 2:1–11) was at the wedding in Cana, when He turned water into wine. And someday, in His timing, Jesus will come back as the Bridegroom for His Bride, the Church. "Let us rejoice and be glad and give the glory to Him, for the marriage of the Lamb has come and His bride has made herself ready" (Revelation 19:7).

The Third Dream: Treasure of Heaven

The third dream, of a royal wedding, followed the theme of marriage. The Father and the Son came to my house as the commanders of heavenly armies. They wore red, representing warfare, passion and the blood of the Lamb. I was reminded of Isaiah 63:1–2:

> Who is . . . this One who is majestic in His apparel, marching in the greatness of His strength? "It is I who speak in righteousness, mighty to save."
> Why is Your apparel red, and Your garments like the one who treads in the wine press?

They were rejoicing because of the wedding that was about to take place. Indeed, they were coming to my parents' house to bring the dowry for the bride.

"We have a gift for you," the Father said when I opened the door, presenting me a big treasure box like the Ark of the Covenant. "It is the most precious gift."

I was so excited, wondering what it was, but they told me it was a surprise.

When they opened it for me, I was hit with the Shekinah glory of God. The box contained a beautiful, bright, shining light. "Here," they said, "the treasure of heaven—the Holy Spirit."

As I realized what the gift was, I understood that the Holy Spirit will prepare the Church for the wedding day with our beloved Bridegroom, Jesus.

When I started my fast, the Lord had told me that when Jesus began His fast, He was filled with the Holy Spirit. But when He finished, He was filled with the *power* of the Holy Spirit. Luke 4:14 says, "Jesus returned to Galilee in the power of the Spirit, and news about him spread through the whole countryside" (NIV).

I had been fasting for the power of the Holy Spirit, and the Father and Son were bringing it to me. I longed for an outpouring of the Holy Spirit like in Joel 2:28: "I will pour out my Spirit on all people. Your sons and daughters will prophesy, your old men will dream dreams, your young men will see visions" (NIV).

In my dream I was weeping. I had been praying for the increased power and presence of the Holy Spirit, and the Lord had heard me. My heart had been made tender through my fast.

The Fourth Dream: Diamonds and Precious Stones (1 Peter 2:4–9)

The final dream was at the end of the fast. I saw treasure on the ground in the shape of a cross made out of diamonds and precious stones, which were a turquoise blue. Next to the cross some Asian ladies wore the same turquoise blue–colored clothes, very expensive, like princesses. They were sitting on the ground, looking down at the cross.

I woke up confused, not sure what the Lord was saying. Later that day, when I was sharing the dream with a friend, she told me I must meet a friend of hers who had recently come back from a trip to Asia. When I met him, he told me of his experience. He had traveled all over Asia preaching the Gospel, and everywhere they went, diamonds appeared. He felt it was a gift for the Asians, because Jesus loves them so much.

Diamonds represent a priestly calling. The priests in Exodus 28 and Leviticus had stones on their garments as part of the tribes of Israel. After that I found a set of three diamond rings—an engagement ring, a wedding ring and an anniversary ring—from my beloved Bridegroom.

At the same time as I met my Asian friend, I was introduced to other Asian Christian leaders from the underground church. The church in Asia is now the biggest in the world. Many of the Christians now taking the Gospel to Israel are coming from the East, through the Silk Road.

I sensed this was what God had been showing me in the dream. The Asian church, even though it is persecuted, will lead the way as we prepare the way for the coming of the Lord.

Faithful to His Promises

Looking back over my years of personal persecution, and the persecution of the Church in my country, I see that it was a precious gift to us—to refine us, to prune us to bring more fruits and to draw us very close to our Maker. It allowed us to grow—just as the church in Jerusalem grew and spread throughout the world when it was persecuted.

He sustained us through it and showed me He is faithful to His promises. Persecution is a blessing that made my faith as gold. It made a mess a message, a test a testimony, a trial a triumph and my greatest weakness my greatest strength!

My mandate on earth now is to wake up the Church and to encourage Christians to speak of the Good News—that Jesus is the only way to the Father, and through Him we have eternal life. Coming from a Muslim background, I have a burden for Muslim nations, but many Christians are fearful to go and share their faith. I encourage you to start praying for them. Through prayer, you will have a heart for them. Pray, "Lord of the harvest, send out laborers," and be ready to be the answer to your own prayer.

There are common reasons Christians don't evangelize Muslims: the fear of what Muslims will do to them and the fear of dying. Also, many feel they don't know enough about Islam to be able to answer questions.

In order to communicate to Muslims, we do indeed need to know our own faith and its foundations well. We need to understand why our Christian faith is true and then communicate it. If we start with God's truth, instead of what is culturally different, God will lead us.

If we fear suffering, we won't be effective in evangelizing Muslims. We need to think carefully through the issues of persecution first, before choosing to go to a Muslim country. But the Bible was written *by* persecuted Christians *to* persecuted Christians *for* persecuted Christians.

Finally, many Christians don't go to evangelize Muslims because we aren't obeying what Jesus said—to make *disciples* of all nations. We can preach to a thousand, but if we don't disciple them, we didn't obey Jesus.

> **The Bible was written by persecuted Christians to persecuted Christians for persecuted Christians.**

We are responsible to replace all the lies with the truth. How? By preaching God's love and truth. When you know His truth, you will recognize the deception. It is only when you know light that you can discern the darkness!

But we must not forget that Jesus is always with us—through every situation. I know, with all my being, that Jesus is always with me. He sustains me.

In fact, I had a dream a while ago that I was dancing with Him in a castle, which I assume was the New Jerusalem.

Jesus is and was and will be the Lover of my Soul, romancing me in His arms of love. I know His love, and I function out of His love.

He is worth it all.

Will you give Him your all?

Samaa Habib grew up in an Islamic family in the Middle East. From an early age she had a desire to know God and became a dedicated Muslim as a child. Her life was radically transformed when she encountered the love of Jesus through a dream and a vision in her teenage years. After her baptism as a Christian believer, she faced persecution on a regular basis, culminating in a terrifying bomb attack on her church fellowship where she had a death experience. The heavenly face-to-face encounter she had with Jesus during her death experience has left an indelible mark on her life. It ended with Jesus commissioning her to come back and tell the world He is real and coming again soon. Since that time, Samaa has traveled the world, sharing her incredible testimony of converting from Islam to Christianity. Her inspirational story of God's love, radical forgiveness, reconciliation and the power of the Holy Spirit is a powerful reminder that we do not serve the god of hatred; we serve the God of love! Her life calling is to encourage the Church to be an ambassador of Christ's love, to prepare the Bride of Christ for the return of the Lord and to remind us all to live for eternity with heaven's view.

Bodie Thoene (pronounced *Tay-nee)* has written over sixty-five works of historical fiction. That these bestsellers have sold more than thirty-five million copies and won eight ECPA Gold Medallion Awards affirms what millions of readers have already discovered—that Bodie and her husband, Brock, the other essential half of the writing team as researcher and consultant, are not only master stylists but experts at capturing readers' minds and hearts.

In their timeless classic series about Israel (The Zion Chronicles, The Zion Covenant, The Zion Legacy, The Zion Diaries), the Thoenes' love for both story and research shines. With The Shiloh Legacy and *Shiloh Autumn* (poignant portrayals of the American Depression), The Galway Chronicles (dramatic stories of the 1840s famine in Ireland) and the Legends of the West (gripping tales of adventure and danger in a land without law), the Thoenes have made their mark in modern history. In the A.D. Chronicles they stepped seamlessly into the world of Jerusalem and Rome, in the days when Yeshua walked the earth, and have continued that journey in the Jerusalem Chronicles through the most crucial events in the life of Yeshua.

Bodie, who has degrees in journalism and communications, began her writing career as a teen journalist for her local newspaper. Eventually her byline appeared in prestigious periodicals such as *U.S. News and World Report, The American West* and *The Saturday Evening Post*. She also worked for John Wayne's

Batjac Productions and ABC Circle Films as a writer and researcher. John Wayne described her as "a writer with talent that captures the people and the times!"

Bodie and Brock have four grown children—Rachel, Jake, Luke and Ellie—and eight grandchildren. Their children are carrying on the Thoene family talent as the next generation of writers, and Luke produces the Thoene audio books. Bodie and Brock divide their time between Hawaii, London and Nevada.

www.thoenebooks.com
www.familyaudiolibrary.com